HERE FOR A REASON

By

Carol Lisle
as told to Vanessa Morgan

Grosvenor House
Publishing Limited

All rights reserved
Copyright © Carol Lisle, 2025

The right of Carol Lisle to be identified as the author of this
work has been asserted in accordance with Section 78
of the Copyright, Designs and Patents Act 1988

The book cover is copyright to Carol Lisle

This book is published by
Grosvenor House Publishing Ltd
Link House
140 The Broadway, Tolworth, Surrey, KT6 7HT.
www.grosvenorhousepublishing.co.uk

This book is sold subject to the conditions that it shall not, by way of
trade or otherwise, be lent, resold, hired out or otherwise circulated
without the author's or publisher's prior consent in any form of
binding or cover other than that in which it is published and
without a similar condition including this condition being
imposed on the subsequent purchaser.

A CIP record for this book
is available from the British Library

ISBN 978-1-83615-278-1

Contents

Foreword	vii
Growing up	1
Married life	13
Learning to live with spirit	22
My castle home	39
There is good and there is bad	58
Home and family	73
Regression	92
Paranormal investigations	104
Spirits in the night	119
Spirit world	139
Spirits and their loved ones	171
A meeting with an extraordinary woman	190
Spirit guiding my pen	204
One final experience	218

"If I am here for a reason.
I want that reason to be to show there is a spirit world.

My desire for this book is to prove that there is life after death and that people can see it and say, there is something. And if it brings someone comfort or hope that's all I want. I just want people to know that when they go over it's a lovely place to be. And I do believe we are reborn again. If ten people read it and feel – I know my mum's all right, I know everyone's all right, I'll be happy."

The card of happiness and wishes

Foreword
by
Cordelia, a regular visitor

"After losing my father in difficult and unexpected circumstances, grief, loss and shock were all things I knew I had to work through as many people do. One of the things that surprised me, was the worry I felt for him and the fact I felt stricken, often when it came thinking if he was ok. As someone who has been brought up by two parents, one of whom grew up Catholic and one who was an atheist, I often felt torn in my beliefs and had in my life been drawn to spirituality.

About six months after my father had passed away I described these feelings of worry to a friend, and articulated it may be wrapped up in the trauma of losing him suddenly and not having had time to say goodbye. So it was recommended that I went to see Carol although I was somewhat sceptical and apprehensive of the reading I tried to keep an open mind.

Carol made me feel at ease from the off as she didn't want to take any personal details, even my surname, when I made the booking. She also never asked for details from me throughout the reading or hung leading statements in the air.

My father came through in the reading and it was unbelievably accurate.

Having been to other people for readings in the past, who gave vague allusions to things that could be meaningful, this was like nothing I had ever experienced or even seen in films. With no hesitation in her voice, throughout the reading, Carol gave me all of my immediate family members names, dates of birth, my father's name, what we used to shorten it to, the pet name he called my mother, his sister and mother's names, my older brother's wife's name, his doctor's name, exactly what he died from, the date he died, my then husband's name, where we lived, where we had booked to go on holiday, the colour of the pillows in my sitting room (which I had been finding on the floor regularly after Dad died), personality profiles of my brothers that were bang on and used my Dads sort of language, the fact my brother would go on to have two little girls, my mums birthday, the fact I hadn't told her I was going to the reading and was worried about doing so, how long we had been in litigation over his death and what the outcome would be (she was correct), exactly what his grave looked like (it was quite ornate) and many other things.

Carol and my Dad even laughed together about the fact he was an atheist and that this was all quite unexpected – how she could have known that or the fact we used to tease him by calling him Gordy Pordy Pudding and Pie and that he called my mum his little nest of vipers was incredible! It was an absolutely unequivocal amount of facts to be given in an hour long session with someone whom I barely opened my mouth to and who did not know me. I didn't talk very much but I did cry tears of happiness and left the reading feeling a bigger sense of relief than I had ever had in my life.

Following that first visit I went to Carol once or twice a year from then on, whenever I needed to feel connected to my Dad. One time I visited, it was my birthday when I visited both Carol and I were pretty shocked at the fact he asked us to go back out to the front porch where my shoes were, as he had left me a birthday present underneath them. He said we would find a white feather and a black feather – one for me and one for my mum. When Carol and I went back there to look we did indeed find two feathers under my shoe that were a very unusual size (just right to fit in the locket I keep his picture and a lock of his hair in) and one was indeed black and one white. I had been the last person to leave those shoes as I took them off and followed Carol into the kitchen where we both stayed until he told us to look.

I cannot describe the amount of comfort I have gotten out of my visits to Carol. Each time more and more details that couldn't be known by a stranger are given to me. It's like my Dad knows I go there for reassurance that he is still with me. There are many wonderful people out there who do great things in a spiritual setting but there is no one I have ever met who has had such a direct connection to spirit world as Carol. She truly has a gift and she uses that gift for so much good. She genuinely has the best in mind for you when you are sat with her. She is someone who you can trust and who makes you feel safe. She gave me and my Dad back to each other and for that I can never say thank you enough."

Growing up

My early life has always been somewhat of a puzzle and full of mystery. Were my parents my real parents? Was my sister my mother? Was my sister even my sister? Who is the little girl in the corner of a photograph of my mother, father and sister? She looks exactly like me but why am I just standing looking at the family group. Why aren't I standing with them? I look about two years old in this photograph and my sister is, supposedly, aged twelve. But she was fourteen when I was born so if I am there, she should be sixteen. She doesn't look sixteen. So am I there in reality?

It was a conversation with my doctor saying my early years were missing from the records that prompted my feelings of suspicion. As a career I have always been a nursery nurse, I am a qualified nursery nurse. At one stage I had to do an interview for Ofsted where I also had to provide a full medical history. It was then that I received the surprising news from my doctor that they were having difficulty in finding the first ten years of my medical history – "Do you think it's possible that you were adopted?" he asked.

My reaction was that no way could I be adopted. I knew my parents, they loved me, and I loved my dad, my dad was my everything. I felt really upset and sat in the chair wondering what to do. My mum and dad had already died so I decided to phone my sister Barbara. It was difficult because we weren't having a lot of contact with each other at the time. She was with an awful man and because of him she drank too much.

"Hello Barb, it's Carol here. I really need to ask you something," I said.

But she didn't want to talk, making excuses that her partner was due home and she wasn't allowed to talk to me.

"But I really, really need to talk to you. Am I adopted?" The line just went silent and then she put the phone down.

After a short time she phoned me back. 'How the hell did you find out?' she asked, and my heart just sank. "Am I?"

"Well I'm not saying anything – you will find out," was the answer.

A thought then struck me which prompted the next question.

"Is it possible that you could be my mum?"

Silence once again and then a promise that we really needed to talk sometime. But it never happened. It was only two weeks later that I received a phone call from my niece saying my sister was in hospital in Liverpool. It was her life-style and her liver was failing. My father-in-law took me up but her partner was there. He told me I couldn't go in, but I said she was my sister and I was. She hadn't responded to the doctors or anyone but I took her hand and waited.

"Hello, it's bug-a-lugs," I said. Her hand moved. My nieces said that was the first time she had shown any sign of movement. The nurses said she was responding so to keep talking. I did and every time I spoke there was some sign of movement. I had to leave as my father-in-law was waiting to take me back to

Birmingham and she died later that night. All the time she had been silent but just before she died she said – "Tell Carol I love her."

Some time later Steve, my husband, was clearing out the loft and discovered a bag which I had never seen before. I fully believe in transportation within Spirit World and was not surprised to find it was my mother's bag. It was filled with photos, papers, certificates, even her passport was in there and my Dad's old army book.

My niece then gave me some photograph albums which I had never seen before. In fact I had never seen any photographs of me when I was a child. I once asked and all my mum said was "Oh we've got them all here. They're ready when you want them." Now I found the photograph which has made my life such a mystery. But there were other photographs too that have made me wonder.

I'd always gone with the stories I'd been told but I now find myself questioning so much about my life. My sister always seemed jealous of me but I felt it was because my Dad treated me like a Goddess. But then she was always closer to our Mum. Why was this? Was it because our Dad wasn't really her Dad. Amongst my mother's things there was a photograph of a German soldier who my Mum helped while my Dad was away at war. Was there something special about him? I know my dad was in the army during the war. Was he home on leave when my sister was conceived or was someone else her father?

I suppose that is something I shall never know because although spirit may guide me to answer other people's questions I never ask for myself.

I have many traits which my sister had but not my parents. My eye pressure became raised which pointed to eventual glaucoma and I was asked if anybody in family suffered from it. I knew my mum nor my dad never had but then in a conversation with my niece I discovered my sister had. She also suffered from high blood pressure which I also do and yet my mum, who should have been my mum, had no blood pressure and no problems with her eyes. When I last saw my sister she was putting lots of weight on, the same as I'm doing now I'm older. And the more I look in a mirror, the more I see my sister.

According to my birth certificate I was born on the 16th of July 1959 in St Catherine's Hospital, Birkenhead, to William Francis Dutton, a butcher, and Evelyn, nee Jones, who worked in Woolworths on the haberdashery counter. I was two pounds in weight and was always known as 'bag-of-sugar'. My mother was aged thirty-eight and the story I was always told was that my dad had been to Harley Street and paid for one of the first fertility drugs. So if he had done this for me, could he really be the father of my sister?

I grew up most of my life in Birkenhead on a council estate. Our first house was one of those post-war prefabricated houses but the one house I remember really well was the flat we lived in at 40 Grass Wood Road. I had many happy years there.

One incident I remember vividly. It was New Year's Eve and I was aged about seven. We were having a massive party and I remember I was going to be sleeping on a blow-up bed in my parent's room. For Christmas I'd been given a blue cot and doll and I can remember I was sitting in the bedroom feeding the doll. All of a sudden there was a huge white light outside. My dad came in and asked me what I was doing with the electricity?

"Look Dad, look," I said. He looked outside and we both saw the white oblong shaped light hovering outside before it disappeared. The next day all the newspapers were reporting that people had seen UFO's.

It was at a young age, I must have been three or four years old, perhaps even younger, when I started seeing people. Although they were just strangers to me I just used to say "oh hello." I didn't understand what it was. I just thought everybody did it and at first I assumed it was quite normal. But everyone would look at me in a strange way and I'd wonder why. Gradually I began to realise it wasn't normal for everybody, that not everybody sees people. My parents believed it was just bad and wrong and that there was something not right with me so they took me to see the doctor. He said I had a hypo-active imagination and that I would grow out of it. To this day it is still noted on my medical records that I have a hypo-active imagination. After that I was never allowed to talk about it, certainly when my parents were around, which was very difficult because if spirit was in the room and was talking to me I just had to keep quiet and couldn't answer them.

The worst time I found was between the ages of 13 and 19. I used to get voices in my head and did become quite scared. I couldn't even turn a corner without somebody being there and telling me things. Sometimes, something, a thought, would just come into my head and then it would happen. As a kid that was quite scary, but now, of course, I know what it's all about.

I went to Noctorum Girls High School in Birkenhead. It was classed as quite a posh school, being an all-girls school, but it wasn't really. I hated school and my attitude was, if I didn't want to do something, I wasn't going to do it. So now the school also thought there was something wrong with me and asked my parents to attend a meeting. Eventually it was decided I might be dyslexic so from then on I was put at the back of the class and as happened in those days was expected to just get on with it.

As a family we went to the Isle of Man every year for our holiday and every year I wanted to go to the witchcraft museum. It was like an antique shop but all witchified. An amazing place which as a child absolutely fascinated me. It was a place I felt I could really talk to people. My mum and dad would sit having tea or coffee, or whatever, outside and I'd walk round the museum. I loved that place. For me it was like I'd been put in a sweetshop. I could feel a presence and hear all these voices talking to me. I've always loved anything to do with witches. I've even got a broomstick in my kitchen which came from an original witch's cottage. I saw it in Ludlow market and the lady said she would only sell it to whoever she thought was the rightful owner. I loved it. It had even got witch's fingers around the base of the brush. She wanted £35 for it but I'd only got £12 in my purse. She looked at me and then said – "Are you a medium?" When I said I was she let me have it.

I always used to say to my husband Steve "if there's one place in the world I would love to go back to, it's the Witchcraft Museum." Then one year we had a family holiday in Cornwall and I couldn't believe my eyes when I saw the museum had moved to Boscastle. It was after they had had the floods and there were sandbags everywhere. Half the museum had been ruined because of the floods but again I was like a kid in a sweetshop. The guy there commented on how fascinated I was and I told him I'd been to the one on the Isle of Man. As we got chatting I found out he was the owner and that it was his dad who had the one on the Isle of Man. When his father had retired, and he had taken over the museum, he had moved all the artefacts and exhibits from the Isle of Man to this new museum in Boscastle.

But what I remember from when I visited as a child was that, when I walked in, the whole place seemed to come alive. The owner was very much into witchcraft and on one occasion, seeing how interested I was, asked me to rub an ornament and when I did he said "you'll have some luck." My dad laughed about it but later when we went into an arcade and settled down to play bingo I wiped them out. I just kept winning all the time, and my dad joked telling me to – "go back and rub that thing again."

By the time I was sixteen I hadn't grown out of my 'so-called' hypo-active imagination, as my parents had hoped, so my dad decided the best thing was to have me examined in an asylum. I was even certified because that's the thing that happened at the time. You see years ago people didn't understand all this spiritual stuff. I sometimes think, if I'd have been born hundreds of years ago, I'd probably have been burnt at the stake.

My dad kept saying there was something wrong with me, that I wasn't right in the head, so they gave me a thorough examination. Testing me for seizures or epilepsy, all sorts, and I had to sit with contraptions on my head while the doctors tried to find out what was wrong. Naturally they couldn't find anything wrong. It was something I was born with and has stayed with me. I can remember always being told – "you'll be alright, you're here for a reason." And that is how I've lived my life. That feeling that I'm here for a reason.

I've led a charmed life. Again I feel that is proof that I'm here for a reason and that I have work to do.

As a child I suffered two close fatalities. One Saturday when I was aged 10 I was playing near my home with my friend Karen, and I remember the sky turning a really funny colour then I don't remember anything else, just this horrendous pain up my leg and my bottom, and then waking up in hospital. I'd been struck by lightning.

When I was twelve I fell off the horse box while doing gym at school and shattered my ankle. I ended up with plaster-of-Paris and just sitting around at home. But then one day I started to feel really ill, my head hurt and I couldn't look at any lights. They called the doctor and he had me admitted to hospital. Tests showed I'd got meningitis. I remember having the lumbar puncture, which was horrible, and I remember being in what looked like a prison cell. Once again I miraculously recovered, although I wasn't able to walk and had to learn all over again.

When I was a teenager my sister gave me a Saturday job in her hair salon in Birkenhead. I started by just washing people's hair then as I got older, I became an apprentice hairdresser. This was to earn a bit of money because my parent's expected me to stand on my own two feet. No two ways about it – they made me do it, which is not a bad thing. It's made me the person that I am and I did the same with my girls.

With my first wages I remember buying a pair of tights for school. I also remember one particular Saturday afternoon. When we finished for the day we all used to wash and blow dry our hairs. On this particular Saturday I was in the kitchen finishing the towels and my sister was talking about possibly going on holiday, maybe to Devon or Cornwall. As I listened a voice told me she shouldn't go to Padstow and not to drive along the lanes, particularly in a white estate car or there would be devastation. At the time a white estate didn't mean anything to me as Barbara had a brown Hillman car, so I kept it to myself. A short time later she told me she and her husband had booked a holiday to Mevagissey in Cornwall. My heart sank but I still kept thinking, they've got a brown car. Two days before they were due to go her husband came to the door with a new white estate car. Of course I begged her not to go. Everybody laughed at me, except my mum who had a go at me saying "oh you and this witchy stuff. Stop it."

So off my sister went and when she got to the campsite in Mevagissey, and everything was fine, I thought 'oh thank God my predictions were wrong.' But later she phoned to say that my brother-in-law had had an accident in the car. The car was a write-off. My sister had stayed in the caravan while he had gone out to get something, I presume food, and the accident had happened on a bend in a lane. Luckily he wasn't badly injured.

When I was about 21 I was working in a nightclub in Liverpool called Snobs. One night I came home and going up the stairs I saw a woman standing at the top. The door to my mum and dad's room was open so

I could see them. They were fast asleep so I screamed but then realised they couldn't hear me. I now know that when spirit is around it's pointless screaming because no one is going to hear you. It's a fact that if you're visited in the night and you go to scream, nothing will come out because they have muted you. But I didn't know that then. So I just stood there. The woman just kept looking at me and smiling. Then I heard her say – "Go to bed….Go to bed." So I went to bed.

The next morning my dad, who as I have said didn't like what was happening to me, wasn't around so I told my mum. At first she wasn't interested and said "we've told you to stop this, you're twenty-odd now." But then I described the woman and what she was wearing. My mum went quiet and just looked at me for a moment then said – "No, no no we're not talking about it," and walked away.

I never forgot what the woman looked like and the dress she was wearing and often wondered who she was. It wasn't until years later that I found out. And that was to open up even more mysteries. My mum, as far as I know, was born in Leeds, and her birth certificate says her mum's name was Elsie Rowe. Now Steve's mum is adopted and when we got together my mum and his mum were like a cackling pair of hens. One day we overheard them say "oh well they never need to know that do they?" What 'that' was I don't know but years later my mum was sorting through a tin in which she kept all her big, costume jewellery. Also in that tin were some photographs. So I asked if I could look at them. The first one I pulled out was a picture of a woman. She was identical to the lady I'd seen at the top of the stairs. She even wore exactly the same dress.

As I looked at it my mum just said – "That's my real mother," and left it at that.

I have got a lot of philosophies in which I believe with regards to spirit world. One of them is that we never, ever, die on our own. I do believe that someone always comes to take us over, we never make that journey on our own and I've got proof of that myself. My dad, who never believed in anything to do with the spirit world, who just thought it was a myth and witchcraft and a load of rubbish, eventually did accept what I was experiencing. Sadly it was late in his life.

I worked as a nanny in Spain and after being there a couple of years I had a feeling my dad was ill. He wrote to me all the time and I used to make just one call home a week. That week when I made the call mum told me my dad was very ill. My employer got me a flight straight back home and I nursed my dad through his final days with lung cancer.

One day he picked up his tin of tobacco and threw it across the room saying to me "don't you ever smoke our Carol, and never, ever visit that gin-mill," meaning drinking.

"Dad I'm not going to," I said and gave him a hug.

I sat down next to him on his bed and as he dozed his eyes suddenly opened wide and he exclaimed – "Oh!"

"Are you alright Dad," I said.

"Eh Carol. This rubbish that you do. There must be something in it."

"What do you mean," I said.

"My mother's at the end of the bed."

I asked him if he could see anything else but he said only his mother.

"It's your time to go Dad," I calmly said.

"Do you think so." he said.
"Yes."
"Well I kind of feel I need to." And with that he shut his eyes and left us for spirit world.

Married life

As I've already said I'm a qualified nursery nurse and by the age of 21 I'd met the love of my life and was getting married. He was a DJ who I had met while I was working at Snobs, I even helped him with his DJ-ing sometimes. That summer I went on holiday to Menorca. Now I believe things happen for a reason but when I met a gentleman with two children I didn't know the significance at the time. When he found out I was a nursery nurse he offered me a job but I explained I was getting married the following year so couldn't accept his offer. He said that if ever I was interested in a job I could have one there.

When I came back home, my fiancé decided his career was going to be in Tooting, London, and that the wedding wasn't going to happen. So we split up. It broke my heart so I decided to phone Tony in Menorca and he offered me a six month contract, but I ended up staying almost three years. The job proved to be an amazing experience. I loved it there and of course over all the time I was there I met quite a few people. Then my dad became ill and I had to get home. The only flight Tony could get for me was to Heathrow. So not knowing how I was going to get from Heathrow to Liverpool I looked through 'my-little-black-book,' and I came across a number for a guy I'd met called Paul who came from Sheldon near Birmingham. I phoned him up and without hesitation he said "I'll come and pick you up."

So he picked me up and took me home. We kept in contact after that and then after my dad died I started seeing more of him and ended up marrying him. Looking back now I realise I was on the rebound following my dad's death. At first I was commuting between Liverpool and Birmingham but it got too much so I moved in with his mum. Then we saw that new houses were being built in Tamworth and decided to buy one. Six months later we moved in and I then became pregnant with my first daughter, Gemma.

I am the type of person that if someone hurts me they don't get a second chance. So when I found out Paul was seeing someone else, within a couple of days I was filing for a divorce. I was going to move back to Liverpool but a friend rang me up and told me she was taking me out for my birthday. That night I met Steve. He was with my friend, they had only just started seeing each, and I'd been set up on a blind date with his friend. Me and Steve just clicked and at the end of the evening, when I was walking back to my friend's car, he ran after me and asked for my phone number. I wasn't sure at first, but then decided it wouldn't hurt if I did give him my number. So he found a used match and with that he wrote my number down on the back of a cigarette packet.

I really didn't think I'd hear from him again but he found out where I lived and came over. Ironically he had the same car, a Maestro, as my ex-husband so when he pulled up I thought it was Paul coming to see Gemma. But when I looked I thought "oh no it's that bloke I met the other night," and didn't know what to do. He knocked on the door and asked if he could take me and "the little one out." I was reluctant at first, but eventually agreed. He took us for a drive over to Henley in Arden. When we got there he stopped the car and getting out, said "I'll be two minutes." He went into this a grocery-type shop and came out with a pink hairdryer set for Gemma. She was three years old then and she's still got it to this day. From then on we started seeing each other on the weekends.

In the end Steve said he'd move into the back room and become a lodger and then he eventually paid Paul for his share of the house and we got married.

The near death experiences I suffered in my childhood continued into adulthood and sometimes I just don't understand how I'm still here. I'm like a cat with half-a-dozen lives.

We were booked to go on holiday to Tunisia. Two days before we were due to fly out I said to Steve "I don't think we should go." Of course he asked why and I said "I've just got this awful feeling and it's life-changing." But we went and just after we landed the Gulf War started. Our hotel was right next door to a house owned by Saddam Hussein so we weren't allowed to go out.

It was while we were there I started to feel ill and had this feeling I was pregnant. We had been having problems with me trying to conceive and we were told it might be an idea to undergo tests to see what the problem was, if there was a problem. So Steve's reaction was that I couldn't be. But I was.

We ended up on The Travel Show after that holiday. We had made friends with two nurses who were also staying at our hotel and they both told us not to eat any food. When I looked into the soup there were maggots in it. The nurses contacted the program to say how badly we'd been treated, especially with me thinking I was pregnant. In actual fact one of the reps at the time had turned round and blamed me saying that I shouldn't have gone out there if I was pregnant. The piece on the show was very brief but it did help get some compensation, although it wasn't very much. After that we dropped the case.

At thirty-one weeks they had to break my waters. They were so badly infected they were green and Steve had the horrendous choice of saving me or the baby. He chose me but luckily, against all the odds, my little baby Natalie survived. But it was a difficult time. Natalie was critical and constantly being moved around to different rooms in the ward. Steve, who was not a religious man, went to the hospital chapel everyday to pray for us. We even had her christened at the hospital. Luckily she survived.

On another occasion I went to see my GP and he diagnosed a large fistula in my bottom and gave me antibiotics saying we'll see how you are after Christmas. It was the 16 December 1997. On Christmas Eve I was rushed to the George Eliot hospital in Nuneaton and they had to operate on me. It became a disaster because they slipped and went through my bowel. I ended up having nine operations after that. Which was bad enough but when I was released on Christmas Day after the first operation I was rushed back with septicaemia.

Eventually I was taken on by a wonderful surgeon at Good Hope hospital in Sutton Coldfield and he performed an operation the following August which no one had ever had. But spirit was with me. In the morning while I was waiting to go in for this operation a robin came and sat on the window ledge. I knew it was my mum. My mum always comes to me as a robin.

I was treated like a god in the hospital because basically I was acting as a guinea pig. The operation went according to plan but against the surgeon's wishes I was discharged the following day and all Mr Allen's good work went down the toilet.......... The suggestion was to go to King's College Hospital in London to put a pace-maker inside my bowel, but I'd had enough. I'd had months of nurses messing with me and such-like so I've given up on that now and live my life according to my abilities and the help my wonderful husband gives me.

Somehow I keep bouncing back and it's like I'm on a mission. A mission to prove to people there is something else. That spirit is around us, guiding us and looking after us. I always feel very protected by spirit. Once we were away and I was feeling unwell so went to bed before Steve. He said it was really weird because all the coat hangers in the wardrobe were moving. Like spirit was in there protecting me. We found out later the lodge we were staying in was the owner's original home and his father had died there.

Spirit is both protective and helpful towards me. One Friday I finished work and I was freezing so decided I would have to put the heating on. I went upstairs to the boiler. As I reached the landing I heard a voice say – "Go in your bedroom." So I went into the bedroom where I could hear a hissing noise. Looking at the radiator I could see it was leaking. I got an engineer out and when he looked at it he told us we were very lucky – "If I hadn't come today you whole radiator would have exploded." And goodness knows what damage that would have caused.

Yet again they saved me. They made me feel so cold that, even putting another layer on, I still felt I needed to go upstairs and put the heating on.

On another occasion I'd been out somewhere and when I came home my neighbour from over the road called to me that my alarm was going off. He said not to go into the house on my own so came in with me. We had a look round but as far as we could see there was nothing wrong. No disturbances, nothing, until I went into the conservatory. Somebody had forced the patio doors with a crowbar. I'd got a green carpet and when I looked down, there was just one muddy footmark on the carpet. The policeman who came out happened to be a friend and said how odd it was. Later when they took someone into custody for a series of burglaries in the area, my friend told me that while being interviewed the burglar referred to my address and said 'oh I got in there, put my foot down and something smacked me so hard I ended up on the floor so I did a runner.' He'd told all his mates – "Don't bother with that place it's all weird. I got in, there was nothing there, but it was just like something just pushed me back." So something, or someone, was protecting my house. That story ended up the talk of the police station.

For many years I took the rostrum at Tamworth Spiritual Church with my friend Karen. I also used to sit in a corner and do readings to raise a bit of money for the church. I loved my work there but I also loved the other work I was doing which eventually meant I had to leave the church.

The lady who was running it at the time, Mary, had asked me to stop doing the readings I did at home. She said I wasn't doing anything wrong but she wanted me to work solely for the church. But again I don't like being told what to do so the answer was no.

She also asked me and Karen if we would study for an SNU (Spiritualist National Union) but I didn't want to. I really feel that you can't have a certificate for this work, it's something you're born with. You've either got it or haven't. I've seen too many phonies in my life. For example Angel Cards. You can go to someone who has set a place up down the road and be charged when in actual fact you can do your own angel cards. They were brought out for people to use themselves. Not for people to make money out of.

Anyhow, I refused to do the SNU and left the church. I remember saying to Karen at the time, we're still friends today, that if we go down this route we'll lose our partners and we'll never be happy. Karen did take her SNU and is now the principal of the church but shortly after she started, she split up with her husband. Even to this day she remembers what I said and has said she's never really been happy and wished she'd never gone down that road.

I always know when someone is going to be ill. Or something is going to happen. It doesn't scare me and now with age I think I'm used to it. But it still sometimes shocks me and I always ask the question – "How do I know that?" I knew I was going to lose my friend Lynn. I had given another friend Hazel a reading and told her someone wasn't going to make it through 2021. Hazel actually thought it was either me or Lynn – because we're both her good friends. But it wasn't me it was Lynn. We attended the funeral in July 2021.

Travelling to the crematorium I got it into my head there was water somewhere. So when we arrived I needed to get out of the car as quickly as possible and ran around looking for the water. But I couldn't see anything. When I got inside I sat with Hazel and I kept saying to her "I've been told there's water." As I'm not one for signing hymns I just sat looking out of the window. Then my eyes caught sight of something. There was a small pool of water. I pointed it out to Hazel and as we both looked a feather floated down outside the window. It was a sign from Lynn.

I've been giving readings in my kitchen since the mid-1980's but I've never had to advertise. At first it was just something I did for friends. After all, my job was as a nursery nurse, but then Steve's sister-in-law came to see me bringing a friend with her. Steve's sister-in-law sat down for the first reading and I kept seeing her with an Indian child. I couldn't understand it because she was married to Steve's brother but kept saying to her – "I can see you with an Indian child, a little boy, with the initials J."

When I started her friend's reading I knew something was wrong. This was one reading I felt I wasn't getting anything at all. All I kept seeing was a white van.

"Well I'm in a white van," she said. "What can you see."

"Well all I can see are the doors open and flowers all over the road."

It turned out she was a florist and three days after she'd come to see me she was killed in a car accident. On the impact the back door had come open and all the flowers had fallen out. After that my name started going around and although it was the worst reading I've ever given, it started me on the road to where I am today, helping and guiding people.

But going back to my sister-in-law, she and Steve's brother split up. She met someone else who is Asian and had a son named Jack.

In the early days of my life as a medium myself and two friends also started working unpaid as paranormal investigators, cleansing houses and such-like. Then Caroline Martin from BRMB radio came for a reading and afterwards invited me to join her program. Later I teamed up with a group called Spirits of the Night. Again that was through word of mouth. One of the member's mother had come for a reading then gone home and said "ohhhh you need this woman in the group,"

I have never looked back and my work continues to flourish. In fact my motto is – the day I have to advertise is the day I pack in.

Learning to live with spirit

One of my philosophies is that 3 o'clock in the morning is the time we are most connected with the spirit world. It happens to me a lot. I'm lying in bed and then feel the bed go down, then I feel an arm go around me. And it's no good fighting them off because you don't stand a chance. Probably in the day but not at this miraculous time in the morning. You fight with spirit then and it can become an unpleasant feeling. They immobilise you and you just can not move. It can be scary if you don't know what's happening so I tell people if they have these experiences, don't try to fight it off, just lie there.

Very often they are there for a reason. So when I'm in that situation, which I have been loads of times, I just turn round and start chatting – "Oh you've come to see me. Is there a problem, is something wrong, can I help?" and so-on.

But there was one night when even I was even scared. I was lying on my back and I had this feeling, this overwhelming feeling, and the whole room just felt horrible. It went cold and I could feel myself moving even though I felt I was in a trance. I turned over and for the first time I did scream, or at least tried to. I came face to face with myself. It was a white face, like a ghost, just looking at me. Again I tried to scream but nothing came out. I began to wonder if I was dying, if this was my time. I had never been able to find an answer to what happened that night until during the pandemic. I was really ill following my covid jab and that was exactly how I looked at the time. So I realised that, on that earlier night, I had been seeing myself in the future and wonder now if it was warning of what was to happen.

As I've said I believe in fate. I moved from Liverpool to Tamworth and to a brand new house and then I fell pregnant with my beautiful daughter Gemma. So everything was good. We wanted to enlarge the house and decided to have an extension built. But before the plaster was even dry my husband had gone, leaving me with a two year old daughter. I didn't know anyone, I had no family there, hardly any friends and I just didn't go out. Then I met Steve. I was meant to meet Steve. All that had happened to me led up to that point.

At first he wasn't a believer, it's 'seeing is believing' with Steve, but I decided this time I wasn't going to hold it back. I'd lost my first husband because of it and my parents didn't want me to do it, but I know that I'm here for a reason so this time I was going to be honest from the beginning. And we haven't looked back since.

We got married on the 15th of July 1989 and I'd chosen a beautiful ring but when I went to put it on, it split. My mum cried out 'Oh that's bad luck, that's bad luck,' and whipped off her old brass ring and gave it to me. So I got married in my mum's wedding ring. The shop I'd bought my ring off were very apologetic and made me another, but it never felt like my wedding ring.

Shortly after the wedding Mum went back to Liverpool and ironically, two days after she got back, her wedding ring went missing. It has never been found to this day. The only time she had ever taken it off was on my wedding day, but somehow it had just disappeared. So she got herself another ring, a thick band with striped engravings on. After mum died and I was visiting my sister she said that I could have this ring. I thought I'd wear it as a thumb ring but when I put it on, it felt slightly too big. I wondered whether to have it altered or not. I always think that if you have jewellery altered you take away the sentiment, but then I thought if I didn't, it would just sit in a box and I was sure my mum wouldn't mind me having it altered. So I went to a jeweller's in town and asked if there was any way it could be made smaller. They said yes no problem but they would have to send it away and it would take about a week. A week later they phoned me and asked me if I could go into the shop because they preferred to speak to me in person. When I went in the assistant said I'm really sorry but your mum's wedding ring – it's split. I knew I shouldn't have had it altered and that was my mum's way of telling me so. She had made it happen.

As a gesture the shop had another one made for me, but it just didn't mean anything to me so I eventually sold it. That's so typical of me. Anyone else would have just had it fixed and no problem, but not me.

Even my marriage certificate isn't what it should be. I really don't know if it's a legal document? We were married on the 15th of July and the following day, the 16th, is my birthday. When we re-took our marriage vows I took my marriage certificate in case it was needed and it was then discovered the date on it was the 16th not the 15th. We always joke saying I can't do anything right so there will probably even be something unusual about my death.

As I said Steve wasn't a believer when we first met and it was a visit to Pendle Hill in Lancashire which really convinced Steve.

Pendle Hill is well known for the witch trials which took place in 1612 and where twelve local women were accused of killing ten people by using witchcraft. One, who was an elderly woman in her eighties, died in gaol before the trial, another turned witness so was released but the other ten were all found guilty and hanged. They are said to still haunt the area and local people are afraid to visit the hill at night where mystery figures have been seen moving around its slopes.

So it was certainly a place I wanted to visit. I'd been asked to attend an event in that area which had been cancelled at the last minute but with the hotel having been booked it was too good an opportunity to miss. So we decided to still go up there.

When we arrived in Pendle we went into an old pub for a drink first and I sat by an old fireplace. Apparently one of the 'witches' used to visit the inn all those years ago. Opposite was the museum so afterwards we decided to go and have a look around there. The man on the door welcomed us and invited us to go upstairs saying there was no one else up there. We had a good look around and listened to the audio equipment and watched the video tapes and found it all very interesting. Before going back downstairs we stood looking out of the window at the pub opposite. As we chatted a man came into the room. He could see how interested we were so Steve told him it was my job and that I just loved anything to do with witches. The man then pointed out a picture and was telling us who all the individuals were in the picture. I asked who was the man in the middle.

"Oh that's a brother of the witch's," he said and then added "Oh but you've seen his sister at the pub."

Steve told him we didn't talk to anyone in the pub. But he was insistent – "oh but you did." We looked at each other then turned back to him. But he had disappeared.

Back downstairs we told the man on the door how much we'd enjoyed our visit and that the other gentleman upstairs had given us so much information.

"But there's been no one up there," he said.

"Well I've just spoken to him." Steve argued. But the man insisted no one else had been up there.

As we left Steve looked at me and said, "Have we just spoken to a spirit?"

I laughed and said, "looks like it, Steve."

When Steve's photographs were developed we spotted something strange. On one, which he had taken of me in the pub, there was a face at the side of me looking out from the wall. It is the exact image of one of the witches from drawings I have seen.

Over the years Steve and I have visited some wonderful places and all of them seem to have stories of their own.

One of our favourite places is Longnor Wood in the Peak District. We go there regularly and were actually booked to go in April 2020 but of course, because of Covid, it was postponed until the October. Then cancelled again and it wasn't until a year later in October 2021 that we eventually got there.

On the Thursday night prior to us travelling up on the following afternoon I had a dream. I kept dreaming about a white owl with huge eyes. It was everywhere I went.

We arrived at Longnor about four in the afternoon and found the lodge where we always stay had been completely renovated. But, as always, I found it very atmospheric and spooky. That evening we had booked to go to a pub called The Winking Man. Being up on the peaks, as the mists descend, it does become quite eerie and this particular evening was no exception. As we drove across the moor we both noticed something white in our peripheral vision. When we looked we could see there was a white bird flying along side the car. We were sure it was a white owl.

On the way back it was getting quite misty and when we got to that same spot a white object suddenly just flew straight across the front of the car. Although we both shouted 'what on earth was that!' we both thought it was the white owl again.

On the second evening we decided to go to a different pub, The Royal Oak in Hurdlow. This place is in a different direction to The Winking Man but we still had to drive across the moors and along narrow country lanes. As we turned around a corner there, in front of us, sitting on a fence, was a great big white owl.

We have been going so regularly to these lodges in Longnor that we have become very friendly with the owner, John, and his family. The following day we were talking to their son and he told me that there had recently been sightings of white owls which had never been seen before.

That evening we went back to the Winking Man and as we pulled out onto the lane, there in the trees, was a white owl. I couldn't believe it but then on the way back, once again, straight across the windscreen flew a white owl. We've been to Longnor I don't know how many times and have never seen owls of any description before.

In my book of dreams, dreaming of a white owl is a good omen. White owls are a promise of success in all that you do. Spiritually they signify change and transformation and if one flies in front of you it's a sign that you mustn't ignore opportunities that may come your way in order to bring change in your life for the better.

At the time I had just started writing this book and Steve commented that this might be significant.

"This book is going to be about you, and you proving to everybody out there that there is something," he said. "You've got that passion."

So maybe the owl was showing me that this is it – this is my success. Proving to people there is life after death. That we don't just go to nothing. That our souls are there.

When staying at Longnor we always visit Chatsworth House, one of England's famous stately homes. A wonderful place with lots of history, the original estate having been bought by Sir William Cavendish in 1549. Sixteen generations of the Cavendish family who, since 1694, have been the Dukes of Devonshire have lived there.

A second house was built in the early 1700's but the original house still stands up on the hill overlooking it and Bess of Hardwick, the wife of Sir William Cavendish, is said to wander around the house at night. But she is only one of several others which have been seen over the years. Included in these is Mary Queen of

Scots who spent some time here during her captivity. Others include a transparent figure which drifts around the library as if searching for a book on the shelves. And a screaming woman has been seen on the bridge who is supposedly someone who witnessed her child being drowned in the water below.

Unfortunately I can't say that I have seen any of these but I do feel a presence there. On one visit we were in the room they call the 'Room of Wealth'. This room is where they display all the valuables they have acquired or had made. While in this room we took lots of photographs and this brings me to one of my latest philosophies. The most amazing thing with modern technology now is that spirit can transport themselves into photographs as coloured lights and such-like, even figures. So it was no surprise to see in the Room of Wealth photos, coloured orbs of light dotted over them showing the spirits which are in that room protecting all the valuables.

I don't drive but I can say to Steve there's something wrong with the car and the next minute we've got a problem with the car. Sometimes I don't feel comfortable in a car. I get a wrenching sickly feeling in my stomach and I will say to Steve "Oh I don't feel right." The next thing we hear there's been an accident or problem either behind us or up in front. Once we were going through Chirk on our way to Ruthin. Although Steve's not a fast driver I felt I needed to tell him to slow down.

"I think something is going to run in front of you." I said.

The next thing a black cat ran out into the road. So I do get feelings that something is going to happen. But one experience we had with a car I won't forget easily.

For my 55th birthday we booked to go to Scotland, a place I had always wanted to go because I love deer and wanted to be close to them. We booked a lodge for a week in the little village of Whitebridge called Otter River View. It was beautiful and was set right over the River Fechlin, ten miles from Loch Ness but miles from the nearest shop. This trip had been planned for twelve months. We'd planned everything and were due to go on the 14th of May 2015. To break the journey on the way up we had also booked one night at the Blacksmith's Hotel in Gretna Green.

Steve decided it would be cheaper to hire a car rather than use his mileage up, something we have done before, but we stipulated we didn't want a red car. Steve will never have a red car. It's just a superstition. Every time he's been in a red car there's been some sort of incident or accident. So we arranged to have either a Focus or an Insignia of any colour except red. On the morning, at a quarter to nine, the hire company turned up with a red car. Steve said "I'm not even attempting to drive this car you can take it back to the office." So they took it back.

Now the night before I'd had a dream. I was sitting in a blue car and we were travelling in horrendous weather conditions. Suddenly we had a terrible accident where something came flying towards us. I woke up in quite a sweat and I was told not to get into that car. I described it to Steve and he said it sounded like a Skoda.

"Well," I said, "we're in this car and we're going to die."

When Steve and the guy came back from the car hire place to my shock, when I looked out of the window, there was a blue car and it was a Skoda Octavia.

"No, no I'm not having that!" I said.

The guy looked at me but I begged him to change it.

He said "I'm sorry but we've got no more cars, you'll have to have it."

Steve said we'd got no choice and told me not to worry.

When we left at two minutes past nine in the morning it was starting to rain and I felt really uncomfortable in this car. Steve kept telling me to stop worrying and that we'd be fine but then the weather got worse. We had just got onto the M42 and were heading for the next junction when, all of a sudden, just before the junction, we could see something hurtling towards the car. I've never screamed so much in my life. It was a large metal engine plate which had come away from some kind of lorry or wagon and it just missed the windscreen before going straight under the car. You could hear it rip the underneath of the car. The noise was excruciating and I'll never forget that sound for the rest of my life.

Steve pulled onto the hard shoulder and we got out. The car looked fine until we saw the underneath. It was a write off; nobody could believe it. One of the police officers, who happened to be a friend of mine, said we were so lucky to be alive. If it had gone through the windscreen it would have severed our necks. The car hire firm came out with a little car and couldn't believe what had happened. We did continue our journey and did have a good holiday.

There was another time when a dream involving a car came true. We were going across to Caistor Lakes in Lincolnshire for a short break and the morning we were leaving Steve got up and said he'd had a very strange dream during the night. He said he'd seen a red car and a bus turning off a junction on the motorway and then crash. The bus actually went up in flames. And hovering over the devastation was a mobile phone. Of course I immediately reached for my dreams book. The car meant 'forget luxury' and the red, 'unexpected news and be careful with temper.' But dreaming of an accident was a warning to avoid unnecessary travel for the next twenty-four hours. Walk don't drive was the book's advice. 'If you can't, take immediate precautions or you'll get hurt.'

Well of course I wanted to cancel the trip but Steve said no we would be perfectly all right.

So we travelled the network of motorways across country until we were nearing the junction we had to exit on.

"There, you see, we've been perfectly OK," Steve said.

Then he noticed the woman driving the car behind us was using her mobile phone. Seconds later we were on the slip road and suddenly there was a huge bang. She had driven into the back of us. Luckily we weren't badly injured, I had some whiplash and Steve's face was bruised where he smacked up against the steering wheel, but luckily we were ok.

Theatres are notoriously haunted and I've often felt a presence of some kind when visiting a theatre. Once we went to the New Theatre at Oxford. I can't say that anything happened there but when I went to the toilet, I did feel a bit uneasy. The part of the building where the toilets are was quite old, the theatre having been rebuilt from an older building which had stood on the site since the 1800's. I do remember it feeling very eerie. The toilets in the Alexandra Theatre in Birmingham also have a bit of an eerie feeling. While in them I felt a sense of heaviness. Usually when you get a feeling of heaviness it means that someone's been murdered. But the one for me is the Hippodrome Theatre in Birmingham. Every Christmas Eve afternoon we took the girls to see the panto there. One year we had a box and the whole time I was there I felt someone nudging my back.

I kept saying to Steve, "Stop it, stop poking me."

And he'd say he wasn't doing anything – "I haven't touched you," he would say.

Another time, again strangely in the toilet, I felt I was being watched.

What is it with toilets? There was another toilet which was extremely spooky and this was in Mancetter Manor. You go to the toilets there and you do feel you're being watched. Even my mum experienced something. We took her for a meal there and by then, later in life, she knew what I was doing and knew there was nothing she could do to stop it.

When we went to the toilet she said "Oh it's a bit cold down here."

"Well the heatings on," I said. But I did feel we were being watched.

Back at the table she looked down and made a joke saying "Are you messing about our Carol."

All the knives and forks had been moved and twisted into angles.

"They've all moved," she said looking around the table.

"Yes mum," I said "They're just playing with you."

We often went to a pub in Newton Regis which had been an old highway inn called the Queen's Head. We always sat by the window and quite a few strange things have happened there. Drinks have been moved. We've actually sat and watched a glass start shaking and then slide across the table. There was an old man, an old military man, who went in every night and always sat at the same table. One night we went in and were put at his table.

I laughed and said "Oh what happens if Charles comes in."

I realised by the look on Keith's face that he had died. As I sat there I could feel his presence in that pub. But again there was an atmosphere in the toilets. You had to go down two steps to get to them and people would say "Oh I felt a bit eerie in those toilets."

There are times when I can't even visit friends without something happening.

I have a friend, she is my oldest friend, she's like a sister to me, but her husband doesn't believe and always jokes with me about it. They moved to a beautiful house and we went to visit them in their new home.

As I sat there I looked at him and said "Are you going to Birmingham?"

He said, "Yes."

"Well don't park by that rag market," I said.

"I never park by the rag market," he answered.

"Well don't. But if you do make sure the ticket is stuck on."

Later he did go to Birmingham with a work colleague and did park by the rag market. It wasn't until he'd bought his parking ticket that he realised where he was and remembered our conversation. So of course he started laughing and couldn't wait to tell me that he had parked by the rag market, but that he had got his ticket, so didn't get fined. However he was never able to tell me that as when he got back to his car later, he had got a fine. The ticket had fallen on to the floor so wasn't visible. Ever since then he has no doubts about me and what I do.

During the writing of this book I felt I had come to a point in my life where things were going to change and I was thinking about closing the nursery through the lack of children we were having at that particular time. I've been in that building for forty-three years now and some members of the staff believe in what I do, others just take it with a pinch of salt. One day I was talking about whether I would have to close with one of the girls who doesn't believe. Suddenly there was a thud in the girl's toilets.

Tracey said "Oh it's the wind blowing the door."

"No," I said, "we're in a sealed building."

Later I was standing at the desk and something fell down in the office.

"I heard that!" she said.

The building which the nursery is in, is as active as hell. It was built in 1981 but years before then the land had all been farmland. I did hear that once, many years ago, a little boy was killed on a farm track there. So I often wonder if he is somewhere in the building playing with the toys.

I am usually one of the first ones there so very often open up and I never walk into that building without shouting out – "Good morning everybody. It's only me. Hope you're all well. Let's have a positive day."

As you go in there is a very long corridor and I always turn the lights on as it can be quite dark. Then I go into the main room where all the toys are and I can almost guarantee that I will hear the twinkle, twinkle little star tune. There's a book in one of the cupboards, which has to be opened for it to be motivated, but nearly every morning it sings to me. The girls get really spooked with that and they've tried everything to see if it will start on it's own. Clapping, shouting, all sorts to find a reason but nothing ever works.

We have done experiments in the past. Some nights we have left a little Duplo brick figure out. We positioned him either by the farm set or we'd put him on a shelf, all sorts of places. And when we arrived the next morning it would always have been moved.

One of the girls, Sophie, went to the back door at the end of the corridor once. She specifically asked that no one put the lights out. But one of the girls hadn't heard her, so as she came out of the kitchen she put the lights out. All of a sudden there was a loud bang. Sophie came back down the corridor as white as the spirit that had frightened her. She said she had never felt so cold in her life.

Another time a group of four of us were in the office in front of the computer doing an online course. There are two doors in this room and one, the fire door, is permanently closed so only one is in use. While watching this course we could hear footsteps outside the fire door, getting louder and louder, and the room was getting colder and colder. Suddenly the door opened. One of the girls said it must have been the wind. But as I pointed out – "It's a fire door. Fire doors don't blow open."

Sometimes when we are sitting having lunch, particularly when something had upset me, the noises will be really bad. Sometimes it sounds as if the radiators are going to blow off the walls.

Even the children will ask what the banging is. But sometimes they have seen things too. One little boy would stand by the door leading to the toilets saying he needed to go. I would tell him that he was a big boy now so could go on his own but he would just keep repeating – "No. No. No. No." I would ask him why and he would say it was because of the man. That he didn't like the man. So someone would always have to go with him. Other children would just stand and stare or wave at something. When asked who they were waving at they all said – "the man."

One day we were packing everything up at the end of the day and one of the little toy vacuum cleaners came on on its own and it was singing – "it's time to play, it's time to play."

Another morning Tracy and I were opening up and getting everything ready. As we got on with our work we began to hear lots of rummaging and clattering coming from the kitchen. We ran through to the kitchen and as we got in we saw a cupboard door opening and were just in time to slam the door shut and stop all the glasses from tumbling out.

One day Pete was standing by the hatch when he started shrugging his shoulders and saying "Get-off. Get off." When he turned around he was surprised to see I was on the other side of the room and commented there was no way I could have moved that quick to get over there. He said that someone had touched him on the shoulder and he thought it was me.

"Perhaps it was your imagination," I said.

"No I don't think so," he replied.

Another time he was in the building on his own. He said he'd never been freaked before but this one day he saw a little girl in the hall walking towards the door. At first he thought a parent had brought their child early but then realised there was no one else about. The next minute she was standing in front of him and he said the whole room suddenly felt like ice. He said she was about three years old with blond hair. That she went out towards the front door but when he rushed after her, she had disappeared.

My castle home

Ruthin Castle is a powerful place and has been through the centuries. It has so much history and it is my home from home. We've been going there for years now and the staff always say when we arrive – "Oh the castle knew you were coming." They say they can feel a change in the atmosphere.

When I walk in the first thing I always do, is let spirit know I'm there.

"Hi guys it's me. If you want to talk to me I'm here, if you don't it's entirely up to you, but I'm not going to ask you to do anything. I'm here with the greatest respect for you. Please if you want to be with us, then please be here."

However Steve does sometimes speak out – "Me and Carol are here so if you can, show yourself."

Being an old castle it can be cold, but the warmth I feel is unbelievable. It's like you have stepped back in time, no stress, no rushing around and not answering to anyone. It is also a place which Steve gets more out of than me. He's like a changed person when he's there. Perhaps it's the mysterious phenomenon concerning Steve and Ruthin Castle. He is the splitting image of a portrait in the castle of Colonel Cornwallis who owned Ruthin in the latter half of the 1800's. So I do believe Steve is a descendant of the family. Everyone comments on it whenever we go. The people who work there, the managers, the owners all joke that he's the ancestor of the place.

One time when we were leaving a lady rushed over to Steve and asked if he could stand by the picture. Of course Steve agreed with a grin on his face.

"Are you a descendant of this family?" she asked.

She said she had been watching him at breakfast and just knew she had to speak to him. So he explained our story with the place and how long we've been coming. She had fallen in love with Ruthin Castle and was planning on going back. She wanted to take Steve's photograph with the portrait so who knows, he might have ended up on Tripadvisor.

The first time we went Steve explored the garden taking photographs, something he loves doing. As he was wandering around he felt something cold hit him in the face. Later when his photographs were developed he discovered he had photographed a soldier walking along the nearby hills. Since then he has personally witnessed many paranormal activities while we've been there. Books flying through the air, a little girl floating in mid air outside the window, all sorts. In every room there is a picture of a little girl holding a basket. From our very first visit that picture has intrigued us and we are sure that this is the little girl who Steve saw.

The original castle was created by Dafydd, the brother of Prince Llewelyn, around 1277. It was built from the local red sandstone bedrock from which the town of Ruthin was named. Following the unsuccessful rebellion in 1282, which ended in Dafydd's execution, the castle passed to Edward I and was used by his wife, Eleanor. It then passed to English military leader,

Reginald de Grey, and the de Grey family kept hold of it until the early 1500's.

In 1508, suffering from financial difficulties, George de Grey was forced to sell and it was bought by Henry VII. It was then passed down to his son, Henry VIII, and from then on passed through the royal dynasty until the English Civil War. Desperately needing more income Charles I sold the estate to Sir Thomas Myddleton of Chirk. During the civil war it was a victim of an eleven week siege before it was finally taken by the parliamentary forces who then partially demolished it.

When the last surviving heir of the Myddleton family died in 1796 his estates were divided between his sisters. Eventually Maria Myddleton, who was then married to Frederick West, inherited Ruthin Castle. The castle was then held by three generations of the West family and during that time, in 1826, it was renovated and refurbished to become a palatial country house.

In the latter half of the nineteenth century, when it was owned by William Cornwallis-West and his wife, Patsy, it became a socialite's paradise and entertained many 'celebrities' of the day. These included Jennie Jerome, who later became Lady Randolph Churchill and mother of Winston Churchill, and Lillie Langtrey, actress, socialite and mistress of Edward, Prince of Wales. Edward himself was also a visitor as well as other dignitaries and politicians.

William and Patsy had two daughters. Shelagh married the Duke of Westminster and Daisy, a German prince. Her marriage to Hans Heinrich of Pless was described as a fairytale wedding and the bride's arrival in her new home was celebrated by numerous well-wishers lining the streets for miles. But her happiness did not last. She became a victim of World War One, living in a foreign country and watching her son go off to fight against her own country. Then her marriage ended in divorce and she ended her days living in Poland in what has been described as poverty compared to her younger days.

After the First World War, with the Cornwallis-West family fortunes depleted, the castle was sold and became a clinic which investigated and treated rare medical conditions. The clinic closed in 1950 and eventually the castle went to auction in the early 1960's. It then became a hotel in 1962 and was once again visited by royalty. King Charles III (then Prince of Wales) stayed there on his way to his investiture in 1969.

In the eighteenth century the town of Ruthin was situated on the busy drovers' route between Wales and England and at one time it was said there was about fifty pubs in the town. There is evidence of both Celt and Roman settlements in the district but it was after the castle had been built that the town really began to grow. Castle Street being where the earliest buildings can be found. The name is formed from Rhudd, referring to the red stone of the area, and Din, meaning fort.

During a land dispute between Reynold, the third Baron de Grey, and Owain Glyndwr, the commander of the Welsh rebellion against Henry V in 1400, much of the town was burned to the ground. The castle was one of the few buildings left behind. The first building to be attacked by Owain was the court house which was replaced in 1421. Known as the Old Court House it still stands today and outside can be found the remains of a gibbet. This was last used in 1679 at the execution of Charles Meehan, a Franciscan priest. He had been shipwrecked on the Welsh coast during a time when Catholics were tried for treason. The Old Court House now houses a bank and people have reported that when using the cash machines, they can hear cries and wailing.

It is the ghost of the Lady Grey which is the most well-known feature in Ruthin Castle. When Lady Grey discovered her husband was having a liaison with a local peasant girl she attacked the girl with an axe and killed her. Found guilty of the murder she was sentenced to death and, because she couldn't be buried in consecrated ground because of her crime, her body was buried just outside the castle walls. Her grave is still there today. Dressed all in grey she is said to wander around the castle and its grounds regularly, sometimes still wielding her axe.

Other spirits roam the castle and grounds such as a soldier who wears just one glove and a little girl who has frequently been seen. But as I've said spirits aren't always seen in their human forms and guests are always commenting on the number of orbs which appear in their photographs. Some small, some extremely large. The third floor is the most active. As you go along the corridor you come to a small door which leads to a staircase and which is all boarded up now. I often wonder what is up there now.

Our first visit to Ruthin was around 1987/88. Steve and I hadn't been together long but he wanted to take me away somewhere. He knew I loved castles and one day we picked up a brochure for short breaks in Britain. I also loved Wales because living quite close to it during my childhood we often visited North Wales. Flicking through this brochure I saw a piece advertising Ruthin – 'a castle with a ghost.' I just knew I had to go there and from the minute I walked in, the place had a massive pull on me. I just looked around and knew this was a place I would be coming back to time and again. And Steve agreed with me. I can't explain it, it's just means everything to us. I just feel I'm home.

On that first visit Steve had arranged for flowers to be put in our room for me, and he's done that ever since. That first room was number 304 and it was so old-fashioned. It had got a glass panelled partition which led into the bathroom and on the first night when we ran a bath, the water came out yellow. They sent someone up with a plunger to clear it and he explained how the water from the castle was being carried in old pipes, so not to worry about it.

That first weekend we went I was sure I could feel things and I kept saying I could see things as well. Then in another instance I wasn't sure whether I had imagined it or not. But Steve was getting so much and his photographs were showing so much. As well as the figure in the hills there were other faces and orbs. On one photograph I could plainly see the symbol, which stands for female, next to the portrait of Patsy Cornwallis-West. In another photograph the drawing of a jug appeared on the wall and no matter how many times that wall has been decorated, every time Steve takes a photograph in that room, the jug reappears. Always in the colour which matches the new colour of the wall.

I just felt that every corner I turned there was excitement. Even going into the town on our first evening was magical. Some of the lamp lights weren't working and it was so eerie. It was like everybody in spirit world was watching us.

On our second visit we were the only people staying in the castle. The weather was awful, it was thundering and lightening. Thinking about it I think we must have had every type of weather up there on our numerous visits. We sat in the bar and there was just us and the barman in the bar. He asked us if we'd like a look around the castle. And that was the first time I experienced the real castle. All the nooks and crannies and hidden corners. Rooms that have now been refurbished were old, so old, it was magical.

As I've said Steve often walks about the place on his own exploring and taking photographs. On one occasion he was by the entrance to the dungeons when something white came out of the tunnel and went straight through him. He said it was like a massive orb saturated in icy water. He was certainly soaking wet afterwards. But it's not only photographs that Steve has taken which have had something strange in them. He also once filmed a video. On part of the footage you could see something moving in the background. You couldn't really see the whole of it, or what it was, it was just an arm trying to materialise. On another video a white dove flew straight out of a mirror.

One afternoon during one of our visits there he went outside for a coffee and while sitting there he started talking to the man at the next table. This man wore an old light brown, short-sleeved jacket, trousers and a white shirt and had a Stetson-type hat on his head. They talked about the war, the castle and that he, the gentleman, had been going to Ruthin for years, but that he was on his own. Steve came inside to find me and we both went out to see if he was still there. But he wasn't. We asked the waitress where he'd gone but she said there had been nobody sitting there.

After so many years of visiting Ruthin Castle it seemed the ideal place to re-take our marriage vows in 2014. It was lovely, all taken in Welsh with a Welsh choir performing in the evening and as always, we stayed in the same room.

In the morning we were talking to the wedding coordinator and she said, "Oh Steve, you've cut your neck."

He said he had no idea how that had happened and we thought no more about it. That is until the photographs were developed. As usual they all had something on them. Circles of light, faces, signs, all sorts of things. But in one photograph taken of our bedroom, a sword can be seen floating over the bed. The same sword which appears in the painting of William Cornwallis-West, who Steve is the splitting image of, and which is also in a display cabinet with other artefacts belonging to the castle.

Other members of the family experienced strange things that weekend. After the wedding my son-in-law Leon went up to his room to use the bathroom. He said that as he walked in everything flew out of the shower and bombarded him – shower gels, everything. Then later when we all went up to bed I heard Natalie screaming. When I rushed to her she said there were spots of blood all over the bed. She said she couldn't sleep in that room and the manager found her another. Since then they have refused to visit the place.

Room 222 is a room I am always wary of. We were put in that room on what was probably our third or fourth visit. While sitting down and relaxing in the room after we had arrived I heard a squeaking noise. It sounded like an old, hinged door being opened.

"Stop messing around," I said to Steve.

"I'm not messing around," he said. "Come on we'll go down for a drink."

But then he noticed something. "Did you open this cupboard?"

The luggage rack, which had been laid out for our use, although we hadn't actually used it, was now folded up and lying on the floor. Behind it was the cupboard door. Looking in we saw there was a staircase. So Steve went up to see what was up there. There was a small room which was absolutely full of a huge variety of objects, including an old bath. Written on the bath were the words – 'help me.'

When Steve came down we couldn't get the door shut again so I went down to reception to ask them to come up.

"Impossible," I was told. "That door hasn't been opened in years."

A staff member went back up with me and he couldn't believe how the door had opened. He did manage to force it shut but with great difficulty, then went off to find the key to lock it and we went down to the bar.

When we went back up to our room the cupboard door was open again. It was almost as if they wanted us to go up there. So Steve said he would go. But I insisted he didn't, not at night anyway. We then had a heated discussion about it, during which, somehow, unbelievably, I walked through the bed post and then a book flew through the air.

I had to go down to reception and ask if we could move rooms, that I just couldn't stay in room 222. It was then we went into room 204, Lillie's Room, named after Lillie Langtry, and we've had that room ever since. That is the room I feel I'm most suited to and am happiest in.

We did stay in a room called 'Patsy's Room' once. But I had a problem in there too. I could never open the bathroom door once I was inside. It wasn't a faulty door knob or anything like that because Steve could open it when he was inside. Something wanted to shut me in this bathroom for some reason.

On one occasion when we were visiting, the programme Most Haunted was being filmed there and they were in Room 222. They were using Ouija Boards. I don't like Ouija Boards so didn't really want to get that involved. When using Ouija Boards it is possible to go into a trance and be taken over so I feel I have to be careful with Steve because of what appears to be this connection with the castle. As soon as they got the Ouija Board out I looked at Steve and could see something happening. He was going into a trance and beginning to transfigure. I had to get him outside and slap him really hard.

There was another time when the castle didn't seem as welcoming. We had gone to do a ghost hunt with one of the employees. Simon is a maintenance man there but he's also very susceptible to spirit. He's got a lot of equipment and is very good. Nothing really happened that night but then Simon asked if he could use one of his machines. Which I didn't mind. We were in the King James' Room and he said spirit didn't like men being present, so all the men had to leave the room. That left just four of us sitting in there with the machine picking up various sounds of static and such-like. But then suddenly we heard a crackly voice calling out from the machine – "Stephen Lisle! Stephen Lisle!"

We all looked at each other and one of the girls asked "Are you talking about Stephen Lisle?"

"Yes. Yes." the crackly voice said.

"Do you want Stephen?"

"No. No."

"Do you want Carol?"

"Yes. Yes"

"Why do you want Carol? Do you want Carol is this room?"

"Yes. Yes."

"Why do you want Carol?"

"Nine Eleven. Nine Eleven."

The following morning Tara said to me, "Carol you're booked to come down again in September. On the 11th. To do another ghost hunt."

So September arrived and we went back to Ruthin. However the ghost hunt was actually cancelled because Simon was ill, but we were given the keys to room 222 to do an investigation. We hadn't been sitting in there for long when I started to see Steve's face changing once again. But then something began to happen to me too.

Steve looked at me and said, "you look like you're changing."

"I'm getting out of here," I said. "I do not feel right in here."

I felt that something was latching on to me and when we looked at the photographs later, we could see a massive orb right across my heart. But something definitely stayed with me because the next day, while visiting the nearby Tweedmill Shopping Outlet, I passed out for no reason at all.

I really don't like that room at all. There is definitely something in there because I always feel uncomfortable in it. It's in the oldest part of the castle so naturally there is a lot residue that has been left in there. You could have a roaring fire, but it would still feel cold.

On that visit they were having some of the rooms refurbished and had got numerous rolls of fabrics, and such-like, stored in the Medieval Suite so visitors hadn't been allowed down there for a while. But they did let us go down there. I must say that I did find it more eerie than I ever have before.

As we were walking down I saw a shadow on the stairs so Steve started taking photographs. I then turned round and, although it was dark, I could see a face. I felt like it was breathing in my face. Later when Steve was checking his photographs, sure enough on one photograph, we could see a face up on the ceiling. It was the splitting image of William Cornwallis-West.

I suppose with no one having been down there for a while, and then I appeared, it just got spirit active.

The next time we went back the renovations were still going on and this time we had experiences with the lights in our room. When I left the room I made sure the lights were switched off. When I went back later, all the lights were on. The second time I left, I once again made sure all the lights were off. But when Steve went up after me, they were all back on again. Because of the renovations and some of the rooms being closed I think all the activity was being concentrated in my room. I began to think that spirit didn't like me having to go into a dark room. They certainly don't worry about the electricity bill.

There has got to be bad in the castle as much as there's good but nothing has really ever hurt us when we've been there. For me and Steve there is something very magical about Ruthin and when I know I'm going there, I always feel like a child. It's hard to explain but the minute I enter the castle I feel I'm home and Steve also feels exactly the same. We never get bored or find flaws with the place. In fact the complete opposite. We find a lot more each and every time we visit, even after thirty seven years.

Every time we go there we always get talking to someone. One night a couple came and joined us in the bar and while we were talking to them I saw a ball.

"There's a ball," I said.

But no one else could see it, so I explained I was a medium.

"What colour is the ball?" the lady asked.

"It's blue," I said.

Then I saw a dog.

"Oh look there's a dog coming down the stairs."

As I described it she burst out crying. Only that morning she'd had to take her dog to the vets to be put to sleep and she'd taken a blue ball with her.

Another time we were in the small dining room and got chatting with a couple at the next table. After a while I said to her, "You're a consultant aren't you?"

"Yes I am actually," she said. "How did you know that?"

Steve just explained it was part of what I am.

"I'm really intrigued," she said. "I'm a Covid consultant."

So I looked at the man with her and said "You're a consultant too."

"Well yes I am. But I don't believe in all this," he said.

"You're a plastic surgeon, aren't you?" I added.

He looked at me and said he was.

Their son was intrigued with me. He had just qualified but as I looked at him I felt that he was very insecure and hesitant about what he was going to do. So I told him that he had got to go for whatever it was he wanted to do.

"Don't listen to anybody. Follow your own heart," I told him. Adding that he was to believe in himself and grasp onto whatever he wanted to do. "Don't listen to anybody." I repeated.

He looked at me and said "I really like you. You're very straight forward."

His mother said she could see an aura around me, like a blue light. "A beautiful aura," she said. "And it's been so lovely to speak to you. It's made our night."

Later her son came to find me and to thank me so much for what I'd given him. So I like to think our unexpected meeting helped him decide his future.

Ruthin always finds a way to welcome me. Once we got there really early and they apologised that our room wasn't ready. Of course I said I wasn't expecting it to be and that I was just letting them know we had arrived and that we would go into the bar. There were a few people sitting in there but we found a table, sat down and ordered a coffee. All of a sudden there was a "meow". Everyone was looking around and a lady said to me – "Did you just hear a cat?"

With that the girl brought our coffees over so the lady stopped her and said – "Have you got a cat in here?"

"Oh no. No, we haven't got any cats in the hotel," the girl answered.

"But we heard a cat," the lady insisted.

"It could be a peacock," I said. "Because the peacocks are only just outside."

"I'm sure it was a cat," she said.

A short while later she jumped up. "Oh something's just gone between my legs. There is a cat in this place."

But nobody else had seen anything.

Suddenly for some reason I forgot where I was and started speaking out, telling spirit I was back and how happy I was to be back. There was then a loud bang on the table. The drinks went up in the air and the other visitors looked at me and said – "Are you having fun and games over there too?" The only thing I felt I could say was that I thought I'd knocked the table. But deep down I knew it was spirit giving me a big welcome home.

Before long Kerry came through to tell me our room was ready so thanking her we got up to leave. Just as we did we heard – "Meowww!"

One New Year's Eve we went to a masquerade ball at Ruthin Castle and were really looking forward to it. Everybody was dressed up and we were all wearing masks. The evening was just starting when a lady arrived making a grand entrance. She was all in black, wearing a huge Victorian dress with black ostrich feathers on it. The man with her was wearing a red and gold Cavalier outfit. Everybody was looking at them.

Their table was right in front of ours and I noticed that the couple next to them tried to talk to them. But they just ignored them. I did wonder if she was the actual owner of the hotel, especially as she went out to have photographs taken with the managers. But when I asked one of the waitresses she said no, they didn't know who she was. Adding – "but we think he's someone famous."

As the evening went on they continued to ignore everybody but when I came back from speaking to one of the members of staff, and had to walk past her, she looked up and touching my arm said, in a soft voice – "hello."

Dumbstruck I answered by just replying with a hello.

"That's a bit weird," Steve said as I went back and sat down. "She hasn't spoken to anyone all evening."

Later I went to the toilet and when I came out she was standing waiting for me. So I smiled and she smiled then said "Is it Carol?"

"Yeeees?" I said.

"I'm Esther, lovely to meet you."

"Lovely to meet you but how did you know my name?"

"Because I overheard your good man. And you've been intriguing me all night."

I couldn't understand what she meant as she had been sitting with her back towards me. It was so weird.

I went back to Steve and a little later we got up to dance. While we were dancing she came over and said – "I want your email address. We have a soul connection and I've never had this link with anybody in my life before. But I feel there's a huge attachment between you and I."

She then said she would like us to meet her partner so we went over to their table. Everybody was looking at us and wondering what was going on because they hadn't spoken to anyone all night. Then he got up and joined us on the dance floor and we were all dancing together.

Eventually Tara, a member of staff, came over and said "Your chauffeur is here."

"Ok darling," she said to me, "we've got to go we've got a long drive back to Manchester."

So he came over and gave me a kiss, cheek to cheek, and said "please keep in touch with Esther. She never speaks to people but she feels something with you."

The next day we were the talk of the castle.

Travelling to Ruthin we always go across the Horse Shoe Pass. It's a beautiful ride, with ups and downs, hairpin bends and spacious landscape scenery. But weather-wise it can be uncertain. One particular time we entered it, it was a little foggy. Then from nowhere came the snow. As we had already started our journey we had to finish it. You can't just turn your car around. There isn't room on the narrow, bendy road. It was like all seasons of weather, wind, hail, snow, fog. Then when travelling down into Ruthin there was no snow at all. We later discovered that we had been the last car to cross the pass on that day. Other cars behind us had been stopped and not allowed to continue.

There have been times when weather conditions have nearly prevented us from leaving home but something has made us persevere as we made our journey. A feeling of needing to get there. One December we left home at 8.30 in morning amid forecasts of storms and severe weather. At first we drove straight through with no problems whatsoever until we got just past Llangollen where we could see the water coming down and flooding the road.

There were cars behind us but Steve just said "we've got to go through it."

"We can't," I said. "There's already cars stuck at the side of the road."

"I've got cars behind. There's just nowhere to turn. We've just got to carry on."

I just put my hands over my eyes and Steve just put his foot down. The noise was horrendous but we came out of it and carried on and got about two miles away from Horseshoe Pass. Then the car stalled and as he turned the ignition a great big tree came down in front of us. The people in the cars behind came rushing to see if we were all right. We were but all I know is that if the car hadn't stalled we would have been under that tree.

The road of course had to be closed and we all had to turn around. When we eventually arrived at Ruthin the manager just looked at us and said he really didn't think we were going to make it that day.

I love this area so much I really feel I would like to live there some day. We did look at a property a short distance away once. It was a chapel right on the banks of the River Dee, which still had all the grave stones outside. Looking around I quickly fell in love with it. However when I went upstairs, on the wall in the main bedroom, there was picture of a huge dragon and I just froze. I felt something was terribly wrong. The owner lived in London and at that time it was being rented to a lady who was very much into witchcraft. I kept saying to Steve that there was just something about that place which wasn't right. There was a sadness. But I still really wanted to buy it.

Steve was worried that I didn't drive and that it was right out in the middle of nowhere. I said we'd walk into the village to prove it was doable, so we started walking. It was January and it was a lovely sunny day. But then it started snowing. The twenty minute journey took an hour and when we got into the village everywhere was shut. Steve looked at me and said that if he wasn't here to drive me, how was I going to get food.

"I'm going to break your heart but….." he said.

Even to this day it's still being rented but not for sale now. However one day I have a feeling that it will be mine. The area really does feel like home and as long as I'm in the castle I'll always be happy. Even if I worked there I would be happy. It would be a joy to work there.

There is good and there is bad

There is good and there is bad but I've been lucky and not seen a lot of bad. However, there is one place I could never go back to. It's a place close to Sheffield and is called Mosborough Hall. Don't get me wrong. It is a lovely place, but it just didn't seem to like me. Once a 12th century manor house owned by the High Sheriff of Yorkshire it then passed through many owners, which also included William Carey who married Mary Boleyn, Anne's sister. It is said that it was here that Henry met Anne, while actually having an affair with Mary. Somebody told me about it when I was looking for somewhere for Steve's 40th birthday so I went up to have a look. I went in and was met by this guy who, I have to say, looked just like Lurch out of the Adam's Family. He showed me around then took me to see which room I would prefer.

The first room we went to was right up the top of a spiral staircase and called the Lord John Darcy Suite. It had all the old panelling in and a four poster bed, which I love, but I had a bad feeling about it. It just didn't feel right. Next he showed me a room called 'The French Room'. This one was decorated in green and cream. It was a nice room but I like old things, so felt that perhaps the first room was more suitable.

He booked me in but I came away still not feeling sure about it. There was something about the room which didn't feel comfortable but I did think it was a nicer room than the other one.

The following February we went up but even before we got to the hotel things started to go wrong. As we neared the hotel our car stalled in the middle of the road. Steve was completely taken by surprise, especially when it wouldn't start again. He was there for ages trying to start it. Finally it did and we turned into a pub car park, which was close by, for Steve to check everything was all right. Even though there didn't seem to be a problem, it still wouldn't start again first time. Eventually it did and we drove up to the hotel. I later realised that spirit was trying to prevent me from going to the hotel. Even later I was to realise that other spirits were preventing me from leaving.

It was a beautiful day and really warm for the time of year. In fact we were only wearing t-shirts as we made our way into reception. I checked in and went up to the room on my own. I didn't want Steve to come up straight away because I'd got some wine and a balloon that I wanted to take up without him seeing, so I left him in the reception. When I opened the door to our room it was just like walking into a freezer. It was absolutely icy cold and although the room had big windows and the sun was shining, it was dark. It just felt awful.

So I placed the Prosecco on a table by the television and the balloon alongside it. Then Steve came up saying it was lovely, wonderful in fact. By now I'd got a cardigan and a coat on because I was so cold.

Steve said "I don't know why you're cold Carol. You must be coming down with something because I am absolutely baking."

I felt uneasy. I felt like I was being watched and kept saying to Steve "I feel like people are watching me. It's like hundreds of eyes are staring at me and I'm getting colder and colder."

But Steve kept insisting that it was baking in there.

We went down to the bar where it was a little warmer but I'd left something in the room so had to go back for it. As I climbed the stairs everything felt pretty uneasy and I still had the feeling I was being watched. As I opened the door I had the shock of my life. Something white and cold just flew at me before disappearing. I had asked them to turn the heating up and I didn't think they had but when I felt the radiators they were boiling, absolutely boiling. Then, as I turned to leave, the bottle of Prosecco flew across the room. It didn't shatter but fell with a thud.

I left, went down to Steve and said "I'm sorry but I can't stay in that room."

In fact it was so bad I asked Steve if we could go home. It really was the worst place I'd stayed in as far as spirit was concerned.

After speaking with the girl at reception the hotel said they would see what they could do to find us another room but they thought the French room had been taken. As far as our room was concerned they couldn't turn the heating up any more.

"It is at its maximum," she said.

"But," she added, "you won't be the first person who hasn't wanted to stay in that room."

Then she looked at me and said – "Are you a medium?"

When I said I was she said she would go and check what rooms she'd got available. When she came back she said "Well we won't be having any more visitors tonight."

"Why?" I asked.

"Have you not seen the snow," she said.

"Snow?" we said, then looked at the door and saw we were snowed in.

We both said it was impossible how much snow had come down in an hour, particularly as it had been so warm earlier and hadn't been forecast. So even if I'd insisted, we wouldn't have been able to go home that night. They needed snow ploughs to clear the drive.

"So I can put you in the French Room," the receptionist said, "by Hallow Lane," she added. I didn't know until later what that meant.

The room was green and cream and had amazing drapes. There was a massive four poster bed which had a huge canopy over the top of it. It felt really warm and didn't feel as sickly as the other room. And I didn't feel as if I was being watched. So I did feel happier in this room.

Going back to the Lord Darcy suite to fetch our things an awful smell hit us as we walked in. Even Steve could smell it.

"What is that smell?" he said. "It smells like dead animals, and it's freezing in here now." But feeling the radiators he added "these are red hot, it doesn't make sense."

I didn't want to stay any longer than I needed to and just had to get out. I felt awful. I felt sick and had a feeling as if I was going to pass out. As I left I looked back and the whole room looked like it had been sprayed in blood. I've never seen anything like it before.

I went down to reception while Steve finished moving our things and a woman, who turned out to be the owner, asked if I was settled now and I said "yes but that room has a bit of a character." She didn't say anything. She just laughed. Steve then came down and said to her, "Have you got a black dog?"

She smiled and asked him why.

"Because," he said "I've just seen a large black dog on the stairs."

"No," she said. "That's the ghost dog."

We now hoped that having moved rooms everything would be all right and looked forward to a pleasant stay. We had dinner and then went into the lounge for a drink. But then I started getting a strange feeling that we were going to hear of a death. It was only a short time later that my daughter rang to say she'd been involved in a car accident. Her boyfriend at the time had hit someone and she was in a bit of a state. She wanted me to go home but I said that we couldn't because we were snowed in.

"But there's no snow here," Gemma said, "and you're only up the road."

The man that he had hit later died. It was thought to be a heart attack and so Gemma's boyfriend wasn't to blame. There wasn't even a court case. Gemma always said she didn't know where he'd come from. He'd just appeared in front of the car.

Our short break was getting worse. And it was about to get even more so.

We went up to our room and everything seemed all right but at two-thirty in the morning we woke up and heard people talking in the lane and horses going past. Then Steve exclaimed, "oh my God!"

"What?" I said.

"Just look up," he said.

The canopy over the bed was slowly coming down on top of us. We both jumped out of bed then when we looked, the canopy was back in its correct position.

"Was that just our eyes playing tricks?" Steve asked.

"No Steve. This is the most awful place I've ever been in my life. And I don't want to ever come back here." I said.

There were still people talking in the lane outside but when we looked out of the window there was nobody there.

In the morning there wasn't one bit of snow. It was like it had never snowed. Even the people at the hotel couldn't understand it.

After breakfast we packed up as quickly as we could and left.

As we were getting into the car I looked up at the room and saw someone in the window.

I said to Steve "You know they must have been trying to feed off me."

The snow coming down was them trying to trap me, but the car breaking down was an effort to protect me and stop me from going there. But I hadn't realised.

The owner gave me a book which tells of people being killed in the room that we stayed in. The sounds of horses in the courtyard were the bodies being taken away and those that weren't taken away were hidden behind the panels in the walls. Over the years numerous bones have been found there.

They now use the hotel for paranormal investigations and the French room is used as the bridal suite. Although it's not called that now. But the Lord Darcy suite is exactly the same and people have reported seeing blood coming out of the walls. The hotel advertises a special overnight stay saying – "Are you brave enough to stay overnight in the Lord John Darcy Suite?" Voices raised in anger have been heard in that room during the night and they say it is haunted by the 'White Lady of Mosborough Hall'.

Her story tells of a governess who had an affair with the squire in the 1600's and became pregnant. At first he promised her a small cottage and money but later changed his mind. When she threatened to tell his wife he slit her throat. The angry voices that have been heard are thought to be remnants of their quarrel on that fateful night. The 'ghost dog' apparently belonged to her and pined to death after she had been killed. And as well as being seen, it can also often be heard howling.

A doctor stayed in that room one night to prove it wasn't haunted. He heard nothing all night but in the morning found his bed dripping with blood.

A place I had always wanted to visit was Edinburgh and one holiday we spent a couple of nights in a hotel in Peebles. It was an old castle called Barony Castle with a fascinating history involving the Polish as well as the British. Dating back to the fifteenth century it belonged to the Murrays of Blackbarony who, by the seventeenth century had become very powerful. Throughout the following centuries they held important roles in politics and other administrative roles. Then eventually sold the castle in 1916 when it became a hotel. During World War 2 it was, at first, the headquarters of the Polish army before becoming a training camp for Polish army staff. After the war it reverted back to a hotel. Although remaining a hotel it has passed through various hands since that time. One was Jan Tomaashik, a sergeant from the Polish army who married a Scottish nurse in 1942 and remained in Scotland. After the war he became a hotelier and in 1968 took over the Barony Hotel. During the 1970's he commissioned what has become known as 'The Great Polish Map of Scotland'. Created in the hotel grounds it took a small group of Polish workers six summers to build it. Carved out of concrete it measures 40 metres by 50 metres and stands in an oval pit covering 1,590 square metres. Following a fire in the 1980's the hotel closed and the map was forgotten. Eventually the building was refurbished in the 1990's and when the hotel reopened a fund was set up to restore the map to its former glory. And very impressive it is.

The first night we were there everybody was sitting in the larger room having a drink, but I felt I wanted to go into a smaller room at the side. So we did. I was only sitting there for a short time when I started seeing orbs, lots of them and I said to Steve – "There's a little girl in here." Then I started looking around because I felt there were some stairs somewhere, but I couldn't see any. Steve asked me what I was doing and when I told him he had a look around too before insisting there weren't any stairs. Nevertheless I really felt I wanted to go up some stairs

In the morning Steve went to the reception and asked if the place was haunted. The man just looked at us so Steve gave his usual explanation of what I am and what I do.

He then looked at us and said "Come with me."

"You're going to take us into that small room aren't you?" I said.

"I am," he said. "I am." Adding, "Have you been in that room?"

"Yes," I said. "And I'm very drawn to the turreted area."

"Why?" he asked.

I just looked at him. "Were there some stairs?"

He looked at Steve and said, "She's good isn't she?" Then confirmed that at one time there were stairs leading from that room.

"Who's Amy?" I asked.

"Oh she really is good," he said.

He then told us that a little girl called Amy had been locked in a room up in the turret.

There have been numerous other sightings in this old building. Lady Marie, one of the original owners, can often be seen looking out from her bedroom window on the second floor. She has been heard sobbing and it is thought that this is because, due to redevelopment, she can no longer see all the garden she loved so much or her boys playing there. Another is a housekeeper, Mary, who appears to be keeping an eye on the staff who now work there. A smell of cigars and brandy can often be smelt in one of the lounges accompanied by the vision of a man's figure who appears to be sitting in a rocking chair. Another shadowy figure of a man has been frequently seen walking his dog across the car park towards the wall, leaving a dark shadow similar to a hole in the wall. Blood curdling screams have been heard in the Gazebo accompanied by a blue light. Three girls aged between 8 and 10 years old are buried in the nearby graveyard and the spirit of one of these girls has been seen wearing a blue dress with a white pinafore quietly moving around the nearby trees.

The next day we did a tour around Edinburgh. As we drove around the bottom of Edinburgh Castle it was pouring with rain and as I looked up I said to Steve – "Oh my God!"

Steve looked at me and said "Carol you've gone white."

"I've just seen a young girl being thrown off the castle walls."

We then went on a tour of the castle and we stopped where I had seen the girl falling and the tour guide told us that this was where the witches were thrown off the walls. If they didn't die from the fall they would drown in the water at the bottom. There is an old doorway here, which is all boarded up now, and behind it was a stairway. I could feel that this was where the girls and women had been brought up after being tried in the Witchery and found guilty.

I said to Steve "I feel I'm doing the same walk the witches did all those years ago."

Another interesting place I have visited is Coombe Abbey near Coventry. It is a very historic place. From the twelfth century to the sixteenth century it was a large and very influential monastery, but then in 1539 it fell at the hands of Henry VIII. For the next hundred years it passed through many hands until it was bought in 1622 by the Craven family. The founder of which was Lord Mayor of London in 1610 and supposedly the subject of the story, Dick Whittington. The property remained with that family for the next three hundred years. Coventry City Council developed the park in the 1960's, then after much refurbishment, it became a hotel in 1995.

On our visit we followed an alleyway which led down to the tombs. As we walked through Steve was behind me, then halfway along I felt someone push me. I turned round to shout at Steve to be more careful only to find he wasn't there. He had stopped to look at the tombs so was a long way behind. It happened right by a plaque which told of the connection with Henry VIII so I made a comment about it – "Oh look at that, it could have been Henry VIII who just pushed me," I joked. But my connections with Henry VIII are no joke as you will read later.

I wanted to go back again and stay overnight in the hotel. For some reason I wanted to stay in the Johnson Suite so when I had the opportunity to go to a Medieval Night with some friends, the organiser agreed to book me and Steve into that room. When we got there it was freezing. The hotel put heaters in the room but even then we had to sleep fully clothed in our medieval costumes. I've often said I would like to go back and perhaps sleep in another room but Steve says, "No Carole that's another place that doesn't like you. When we went on our own you were pushed, then the second time we had the experience of a freezing cold room."

In North Wales is another wonderful place called Plas Teg. The house was built in 1610, or thereabouts, by Sir John Trevor, a Welsh politician, and passed through many generations of the Trevor family until World War II when it was requisitioned by the War Office to house British soldiers. In the 1950's, having been left derelict, a descendant of the Trevor family rescued it and renovated parts of it in order to lease it out. It is now owned by a very eccentric lady who used to be an actress. It's an amazing place and filled with spirits. You can go in one room and feel somebody looking at you. In another room you can feel a child push past you. In another room there's just a feeling of eeriness. Every room has got a different kind of feeling. The house also has a lot of connections with witchcraft. There is a beautiful white fireplace in one room and when you look up you can see the witches signs. They would scratch symbols in old fireplaces. Always underneath the marble or at the side. Doing that they put some kind of spell on the place. Not a hex or an evil spell, just one to make it a good place. On the main road outside I picked up that someone had been running across it and was killed. I later found out that people have seen someone in the road at night but when they investigate, there is nobody there. Steve took a photograph and when we looked at it we could see someone in the trees. But there certainly wasn't anyone there when the photograph was taken.

Another of our favourite holiday destinations is Corfu and it was here in the summer following my encounter with Esther on New Year's Eve in Ruthin that I had a feeling of deja vu. We had gone over for a week's holiday staying in Sidari. During that week's holiday we took a boat trip to Paxos. We sat in a quiet part of the boat, right at the front, and as we were sitting there a girl walked past us and then sat down quite close to us, but facing away from us. From the quick glance I had of her as she walked past I thought she seemed very familiar. After thinking about it I decided that she was someone who used to come to see me for readings. I did have an English lady who lived in Corfu come to see me because her sister lived in my area. But I hadn't seen her since before Covid. She must have felt me looking at her because she turned and smiled at me.

"That's Emma," I said to Steve "I'm sure of it."

I didn't think she recognised me so I didn't say anything but I watched her. I could tell that she was also very much a people watcher and that she was taking everything in that was going on around her.

When we arrived at Paxos Steve and I found a cafe to sit and have a drink and enjoy the view. After a while I spotted the mysterious lady swimming in the sea and I just couldn't help watching her.

I was fascinated by her.

"Do you know there is something weird and yet wonderful about her." I said.

When we got back on the boat we found the same seats and sure enough she also came back and sat in the same seat.

After leaving the island the boat was moored up for people to go swimming in the sea. I didn't want to but Steve said he would so dived in. She dived in right behind him, swam up to him and started talking to him. When he came back and sat down he told me he had asked her if her name was Emma and she told him it was Esther. I still felt I knew her from somewhere and then I remembered the Esther we'd met on New Year's Eve.

"It's not Esther, the one we met at Ruthin, is it?" I asked.

"I don't know Carol." Steve replied.

He said when he had asked her if her name was Emma she had said – "No my name's not Emma but it does begin with E. It's Esther."

And she wanted to know all about me.

"Is your wife a medium?" she had asked.

"Yes"

"So am I. And is your wife a white witch?"

"Yes"

"Oh I'll say no more," she replied. So I assumed she was a black witch. Although I couldn't be sure of that.

When she got back on the boat she never said anything to me. She didn't even bat an eyelid. She just sat down on her seat. Although every so often she did look over at me and smile. As we were arriving back in Corfu it was baking hot, there was no wind whatsoever and just half-dozen of us sitting on this small deck at the front. Then suddenly one of the wicker chairs picked itself up, travelled down the boat and positioned itself between me and her. Almost as if someone had pulled it out and moved it to specifically sit between the two of us. I looked at her and she looked at me.

"That's a bit odd," I said

"That's not odd darling. That was meant to happen."

I looked at her and she stood up, smiled and gave a giggle, then just said "byeee" and walked off.

We next saw her standing at the gate to the gangway. As soon as that gate was opened she ran off the boat as fast as she could. I wanted to catch up with her and when I saw her stop in the square I thought we would. But then she just disappeared and I never saw her again. Even now I still keep thinking – was she the Esther from New Years Eve. She did say we should keep in touch.

That wasn't the only strange thing which happened on that holiday. A couple of nights after we had arrived we were sitting in the hotel grounds looking out through some trees over to the pool.

"Why are those two people sitting down there staring at me?" I said to Steve.

"Where?" he answered.

"There's two people sitting on that bench between the trees." I said.

"Carol, there's nobody there."

"There is. There's a lady and a man."

"Carol there is nobody there."

I didn't argue but I knew I could see two people sitting across the grounds and they were both looking at me. One had got leathers on, so I presumed he was a motorcyclist, the other was a girl but I couldn't quite make her out. Anyhow I just dismissed it and forgot about them. And I didn't see them again until the night before we were coming home.

As soon as I saw them I told Steve.

"There's is definitely a couple sitting over there." I said.

But he was adamant there wasn't.

"I can't see them," he kept saying.

"Seriously they are just sitting there in between the trees."

Then they waved to me.

I do know there have been a lot of accidents on the road into Sadari. So I'm presuming, as he was wearing leathers, he was riding a motorbike, but I couldn't really see her, as clearly as him or what she was wearing. Were they both killed on the road together? Or had she joined him later? Answers that will never be answered unless they had wanted to talk to me.

Home and family

It's not just the places I visit, and the people I meet, that have given me such stories. My own house is a source of varied experiences too. However it has never liked change. The minute something is changed we have to have it looked at. You do one thing and another thing happens. None of the neighbours have any problems, it's just our house.

It's like something will warn us. I had some work done on my floor in one room. When he'd finished the workman asked if everything was ok. But someone was saying to me 'look behind the door.' So I looked behind the door and found there was a fault.

Once the lights kept flickering and we thought it was just a bulb going. The bulbs were actually new so we'd turn them off and let them cool down. But when we turned them back on, they started flickering again. And it was like they were flickering in sequence. So when we had an electrician for something else we asked him to look at them. But he couldn't find anything wrong with them.

We were having a new kitchen. As it was the place where I work which was being changed, I knew they would let me know if they weren't happy. It was November 2021.

One morning Steve was up a ladder outside putting the Christmas lights up and Scott, the electrician, had arrived to start the wiring for the new kitchen. We were chatting when all of a sudden there was an almighty crash coming from the living room.

"What on earth was that?" shouted Scott.

At first I really thought that Steve had fallen but rushing to look I was relieved to see he was still up the ladder. Then I looked in my lounge. There on the floor, was a photograph of me and Steve. Wondering why it was on the floor I moved forward to retrieve it but then had to move quickly out of the way. I couldn't believe my eyes. All the photographs on the walls going up the staircase were literally flying through the bannisters, ricocheting and shooting everywhere, before landing all over the lounge floor. There are twenty photographs hanging up on the walls to the staircase and they were everywhere. But they weren't smashed, not one of them, even though they were glass. How did they fly across and into the middle of the room and not just bounce down the stairs? And how did they get through the bannisters? The only two photographs which were left on the wall were of my mum and dad, and Steve's mum. Why were they the only photographs not to fall?

Scott was white with his mouth open. "Oh my God what is happening?" He shouted. "Jesus, what is happening?"

Although he does believe in what I do he still felt the need to go out into the garden for a cigarette and after that he always came into my house very sheepishly.

Hearing the commotion Steve came in to see what had happened. When I explained he just looked at me and said "I think you need a word with spirit world."

I can't even explain that myself. If there had been hammering and such-like going on in the kitchen, which there wasn't, the vibration might have knocked them off the walls. But how could they have veered through the bannister and into the lounge. Also how didn't any of the frames or the glass fronts break? It's an absolute mystery.

And it wasn't the only time that happened. I had a lot of things thrown at me around that time. Or falling down. Things were being moved all the time too. I'd go upstairs and my make-up bag would be on the floor. Or I'd go into the bathroom and my toothbrush had been thrown into the bath.

I'm sure it wasn't poltergeist activity. I know spirit too well and know it was just them letting me know they didn't want any work done in my house.

My house is built on an old mining area and over the years, in particular the early years after buying it when it was new, I've always felt as though someone was watching me. I never told my first husband because he didn't believe, but after I married Steve, I discovered it was a little girl. Her name was Suiki.

When Natalie was born, as I've said, we had to spend a long time in the hospital and while she was being moved from room to room, I stayed in a flat at the hospital. Eventually she was discharged and we came home one Saturday morning.

My mother-in-law had been staying at the house to help look after Gemma and as I arrived home she said "We've been having some really weird goings-on here."

And those 'weird goings-on' continued. For the first week I kept Natalie's cot in our bedroom but then I moved it into her own room. The day we moved the cot I put her down and left her sleeping peacefully. A short time later Steve went up to check on her.

"Where's Natalie. Where's Natalie?" he called down.

"She's in the cot asleep," I said.

"No she's not," he said.

I rushed upstairs and found he was right – she wasn't in the cot. We didn't know what to do apart from frantically searching for her. When we went into the other room we found her lying on the bed. Someone had transported her. This time Steve panicked and said "I'm not having this. I'm not having this." So I called Gerald, a friend from my church, to come and help.

When he arrived it was Gemma he noticed first and asked what was wrong with her.

"Nothing," I said. But he insisted she was suffering from asthma and took her into the kitchen.

"Gemma's in danger," he said.

"What do you mean, Gemma's in danger."

"I don't know but there's something latched on to her."

And with that he started doing some healing on her. Afterwards he said she would suffer from asthma for a while but then it would disappear.

"It's come from a spirit," he said. Then looking around he added, "There's a little girl in here."

I hadn't said anything about what had happened to Natalie but spirit must have told him because he then said, "it's the little girl who moved Natalie."

So I told him to tell her not to do it again and then he asked if I wanted him to get rid of her.

"I don't know," I said. "She must be here for a reason."

"Yes she's looking for her dad," he answered.

It turned out she was aged about six or seven. We thought that perhaps her father had been a miner working in the mines my house had been built on and decided to leave her.

Nothing else happened until a year later.

Gemma developed asthma as Gerald had warned. But as he had predicted the doctor also said she would grow out of it and she did. By this time Natalie had started walking and we noticed that she would always carry two cups around, or two beakers, and when she had a biscuit she always had to have two. Then when she started talking she would always be talking to someone.

"Who are you talking to?" I'd say.

"It's my friend," she would answer "and she's called Suiki."

Because of what I had experienced as a child I decided it was best to leave things as they were and just let them happen.

A few years later Gemma had now reached the age of 18 and one night came home late from her first visit to a night club. We were in bed and all we heard was her screeching "Ahhhhhhhhh!!!!"

"Gemma what on earth is wrong?" I shouted as I rushed downstairs to her.

"I've just seen that girl," she said. "Honestly I'm not drunk but I've just seen her. Tell her to go."

I looked up and for the first time I saw her too. She was at the top of the stairs looking down through the spindles. I decided the time was now right, so I called Gerald over.

"Do you think the time has come to get rid of her?" he asked.

"Well she's been here a long time," I said. "Surely she's still not looking for her dad." Gerald said she was.

"Well this is so cruel," I said. "And every time we have something done to the house we have all sorts of problems. So can we send her back to her dad?"

"Yes," he said and we had a really big session in the kitchen. It felt so weird but ever since then there's been nothing. Until one morning in June 2021.

We heard a lot of crying. Gemma was here as she hadn't been well so we'd brought her over to our house. At first it upset Gemma so I gave her some sweet tea and she sat outside talking to Steve. When she came inside she looked at me and said "For the first time I feel so different about this house. It feels different. It feels really relaxed. It's like someone is looking around here but it doesn't bother me."

There have been times though when Gemma hasn't always felt comfortable with things going on around me. After her granddad died, that is my ex-husband's father, she asked me to go to the grave with her. I always think this particular cemetery is positioned in a very unusual spot. It's just stuck on a spot right by a traffic island and a large supermarket. Of course the cemetery was there first I suppose but it does seem strange.

While Gemma was tidying the grave up I looked around and saw a young lad waving at me. It was like he was beckoning to me.

I said to Gemma, "Do you know that young lad?"

She looked up then said, "Mum, there's nobody there."

"There is. There's a young lad wearing a white shirt and black trousers."

"No mum there's nobody there and you're really spooking me now."

He appeared to be summoning me to the grave so I told Gemma – "I've got to go and see who it is."

Although she still felt spooked, Gemma agreed to come with me.

On my way over to where he was standing I was told his name and I kept saying to Gemma – "His name's Gareth, his name's Gareth."

She couldn't believe it when we got over there and she saw the name on the grave stone was Gareth.

He then told me how he had died in a car accident and that the grave was going to be opened up again in the next twelve months as a family member would be joining him in there.

There have been other times when Gemma has experienced things which have made her think. Only the other day she rang me up to say she had had a really bad dream. She dreamt she was in my house and had fallen asleep in the chair by the fire. There was washing all over the floor in the living room, which she thought was really weird. She woke up very quickly, in her dream, and had a thought she hadn't locked the back door. So in her dream she had run out into the kitchen and found the back door open. It scared her and she felt somebody was in the house. She looked around but there was no one there. She thought she was just being silly but then she looked on the stairs and through the bannisters she could see a face. It was a lady and she was repeatedly saying "yes, yes, yes."

In her dream Gemma ran out of the house and then she woke up.

I asked if she could describe the woman.

"Well she was quite young," she said. "And she'd got glasses on which were quite a funny shape. But

I didn't know her. I'd never seen her in my life before."

Later my grandson was ill and Gemma decided he needed to see a doctor. She was given an appointment with a doctor I had recently seen. Without thinking I said "oh that's the one who wears really strange glasses." When Gemma got there and opened the door she couldn't believe it. It was the woman she'd seen in her dream.

My family have got used to me now. Even in a supermarket I can see someone and Steve will immediately know by the look on my face and my reaction. But I often wonder what other people think? Seeing this woman talking to someone who isn't there. I never really think about that because I just want to acknowledge spirit's presence.

They are also used to me predicting things. I once felt that Natalie was going to change her car. She was looking at a white Volkswagen but I had previously said to Steve "Natalie will have a grey car, a very unusual grey colour. A grey you never normally see. And she will have it sometime in May." One day she phoned me up and said she was in the garage and that she had bought a new car.

"You'll never believe what colour it is," she said.

"It's not grey, is it?" I asked.

It was and it was a brand new shade of grey that Audi had just brought out and was new to the market. And she was getting it in May.

Steve laughed and said, "See, your mother was right again."

But it was only a year later that I was telling her she would be having yet another new car.

I won't do family cards but Natalie had asked if I would do hers. I have to admit I didn't do them properly. We just messed around really but during the reading I told her she was going to change her car.

"Don't be stupid," she said. "It's only a year old and I've got a PCP on it."

A short while later she had a call from the dealer saying they were having a promotion and she had been selected to have a new car at the same cost to her.

During that reading I asked Natalie what connection she had with horses because I could see horses everywhere, all over the place. And resting over these horses was a legal document. She insisted she knew nothing about it and hadn't a clue what I was talking about. But thinking about it she wondered if they were connected to her fiance's father. He was getting married again to a woman who had got a lot of horses.

However a few months later we went off to view the venue for Natalie's wedding and we were greeted with numerous paintings of horses and the most beautiful statue of a horse.

Quite recently I was going into town to meet Gemma one day. I was sitting on the bus and the thought came into my head of 'Tom and bull-in-a-china-shop'. When I got off the bus I was desperate to go to the toilet so we were both rushing. As we turned a corner she ran straight into a man coming out of a take-away, carrying his lunch in his hands. His coffee went one way and his sausage roll the other.

I just shouted "sorry I can't stop, I've got to go," and left them.

When I got back Gemma was still chatting to him and said "Oh mum this is Tom."

He ended up asking her out on a date. Although it didn't become a lasting relationship.

On a couple of occasions spirit has helped Steve with regards to any presents he might be thinking of buying me.

One day, very close to Christmas, I kept getting strange thoughts and was being told me to look under the table. So I did as I was told and found a bag. Inside the bag was my fur coat and I kept thinking 'why is my fur coat in this bag?' Later I went upstairs and there on the back of my bedroom door was my fur coat, where it usually is. So I took it downstairs.

When Steve came home he saw the coat and asked me what I was doing with my Christmas present.

"But you bought me this last year," I said.

"Oh I've bought you the same coat this year."

So thanks to spirit he was able to do something about it in time for Christmas. But even that didn't go quite to plan.

We were going to Shrewsbury and I'd told Steve I wanted some boots – a particular make. So when we spotted a shoe shop he said he was going in, but for me not to come with him. When he came out with a box I thought 'oh good he's got me my boots'.

A few days later the weather was really bad so he decided he would give me my new boots. When I opened them and looked at them I said "Steve these are the boots I've already got."

Later we had a coach trip to Oxford planned and I discovered the same shoe shop was there so I thought I might be able to change them to the other pair I liked.

I rang them up and she said "Oh yes we've got just the one pair left in size 4. I'll put them by for you."

On arriving in Oxford we found the shop but as we walked in she looked at me and said, "I'm afraid you can't have your boots."

"Why?" I asked

"Well you're not going to believe this but I had to get rid of an assistant yesterday because she's done it not only with your boots, but with another four pairs."

She had sold odd pairs of shoes. The left foot in size 4 and the right foot in size 5. So the box waiting for me to collect had two different sizes of boot.

Walking around Oxford that day I had another of my predictions and I said to Steve "you know we're not going to get any food today."

Believe it or not, everywhere we went we were told there was no food.

Steve was amazed. "How did you know that?"

"I don't know. I just did."

When we got back on the coach there were some ladies I knew because I give them readings. They said the same. Everywhere they went they couldn't get food. All the places had run out of food.

I once warned Steve that he had to be careful with paperwork and that he must not sign anything with the initials AH on it. When he was being made redundant there were certain things he had to sign in relation to his redundancy. One was relating to his pension which proved to be a mistake, he missed an important statement in the small print, which effected the way he was being paid. When looking on the letters and forms later there in large letters were the initials of his firm's solicitor – AH.

Sometimes names come to me out-of-the-blue. I once said to Steve "Who's Timothy?" but he had no idea. We had had a holiday booked to Crete which had been cancelled on numerous occasions during the Covid pandemic. Eventually we decided it was best to cancel, mainly due to Steve's redundancy, and have our money back. So I went into the travel agent. At first the agent in the office said we hadn't got a good enough reason to cancel the holiday but, if we could get an official letter of proof of redundancy, he would see what he could do. Which we did, and took it in. Again he just said he would do what he could. But then he looked at our file and saw that we had booked numerous holidays with this company, so said he would certainly try his best adding – "I'm not promising but I'll see what I can do."

When we got home he rang almost immediately and said that head office had accepted the redundancy letter. He then said – "I've been speaking to one of the directors, his name is Timothy."

My sister only ever came to my house once and she didn't like it. We have also never had any cats in our house, but that one time when she did visit, as she walked in she cried out "Oh my god I thought you were allergic to cats."

"I am," I said.

"Well there's a great big cat in here," she answered.

Strangely Steve has often heard a cat meowing. And other visitors often ask about the cat they can hear.

But then there are always sounds in my house.

Something I wanted for many years was a crystal ball. You can buy cheap glass ones but to get a real genuine crystal you have to go to a proper shop. They're not cheap but I really wanted a proper one, so I went along to an appropriate place. It was a small shop in Erdington, Birmingham which sold stones, cards, dream catchers and other witchy things. The first one I saw was only small but I asked if I could have a feel of it. It felt right, I really liked it. I could see things in there, colours, numbers, all sorts. So I bought it.

However the next day I thought that if I'm going to be using it regularly I really needed a bigger one. So we went back to the shop. The assistant was very helpful and said yes I could look at some of the other balls. The first one I didn't like but the second I felt I could work with so I bought it. But when I brought it into the house, the house did not like this ball at all. When I took it into the kitchen it went black so I knew it wasn't right for me. I put it outside then the next morning brought it back into the house. For just the short time I was carrying it, it was burning my hand so I knew I had got to take it back.

The minute I walked into the shop she said, "I knew you'd be back." Apparently it had been returned before. But when I asked if I could have the first one back she said she was sorry someone had bought it. I asked if she would be having any more in but she said it just depended on what they acquired. As I looked around I spotted one up on the top of a cabinet.

"Oh that's not for sale," she said.

Just then the owner appeared and overhearing our conversation said, "Let her have a look."

So she passed it down to me and put it in my hands. When he saw my reaction as I held it he agreed to sell it to me. And it has worked for me ever since. It wasn't as expensive as the larger one I'd just taken back, so I bought another little ball that I had seen and now I have two.

We went through a period when we seemed to have nothing but bad luck. One day I happened to put my hand down the couch and found a small red Buddha. I didn't know where it had come from or what to do with it but I knew it was a hex. So I asked my friend Tracey to come round. She put salt all around the place and thoroughly cleansed the house then suggested the Buddah should be buried in the ground. I felt it should go into water so I took it to a nearby lake and threw it in.

Later we visited Ludlow and went to the market there. Steve saw a small stone statue that he particularly liked. It was a sort of gnome, but I saw it as a gargoyle. He thought it would look good in the conservatory but I didn't like it. It reminded me of the Buddah from before. However he persuaded me to let him buy it.

Once we got it home things started getting bad again and then a lady came to the door for a reading. She was horrified and kept saying she couldn't come into the house. She wanted to stay in the garden but I said I couldn't do her reading out there. It turned out she was involved in feng shui and kept saying "There's something in this house, there's something in this house." Looking around she saw the gnome.

"You've got to get rid of that!" she said. "Somebody is going to get ill."

Three weeks later Steve had a thrombosis and nearly died.

I knew then it had got to go. It had even made a mark on the window ledge which took ages to disappear. In fact there is still a slight blemish there now. First I took the statue out into the garden where we had a lavender bush which was years and years old and buried it there. But the lavender bush died. Someone said the gnome obviously still had its energy, so I moved it to another part of the garden hoping this would remove any energy left in it. I put it under a thorn bush and it nearly killed that too.

So then I wrapped it up in two black bags, telling it repeatedly that it was going to a better place, then put it in the bin. Later I was told that this was a mistake too. I should have either buried it deep underground, deeper than I had been burying it, or thrown it into water. All that had happened was that it had gone to landfill and the energy was still there. It hadn't gone far either. Our landfill is only a couple of miles down the road in Dosthill. The mark it left behind is gradually fading, and the lavender bush came back to life, so I'm hoping the energy is disappearing as the gargoyle gets buried deeper in to the landfill.

People ask me if I have ever predicted incidents which have become national disasters. This has actually happened a couple of times.

In May 2017 my granddaughter was due to go to an Ariana Grande concert at Manchester Arean. I had this funny feeling and said to Gemma "I don't want her to go."

"Mum don't be so stupid." she said.

But I had a gut feeling that something wasn't right. I didn't know what but I was worried. The night before the concert Evie became unwell so couldn't go. But her cousins still went and another little girl had her ticket. As everybody now knows the place was bombed by a suicide bomber. Evie's cousins were ok, but the little girl with them was injured.

Another time I suddenly said to Steve, "What's just hit a building."

"Don't be silly," he said.

We were in the kitchen at the time, but when we went into our lounge and switched the television on there was '9-11' unfolding in front of our eyes.

My dad always said 'don't touch something unless it's broken,' and one night he came to warn me. I'd got my covid jab booked for the following Saturday, which happened to be his birthday, and in all honesty I wasn't looking forward to it. I was sure it would make things worse and I didn't sleep worrying about it.

All my friends were saying – "why Carol? We've all got to have it. You'll be fine."

But I was worried it was going to mess with my mind. What if there was something in it that took away what I've got. I would have hated that.

I had my appointment booked in but during the week prior to the appointment, I kept having terrific dreams. Now I believe in my dreams and look everything up in my dreams book. Also, strangely, in all the years since I lost my dad I have never had a dream about him. But one night during that week I did dream about him. He was there in front of me, wearing the jumper I had bought him before he died, and was saying to me –

'No. No papers on the 27th. Don't sign the papers'.

This made me think of the Covid jab as I hadn't got any other papers to sign, apart from filling in some Covid forms which I'd been asked to fill in by my doctor.

I looked 'dad' up in my book and it said there would be important news, a turn of events, or that something of the past would be lost. I found that intriguing. When I reached out my hand to my dad, a white dog bit it. We haven't had a dog since I was young. He bought it when

I was born, a border collie and when I looked at what 'dog' meant in my book it said – you may uncover a secret that you'd rather not know.

My dad kept standing in front of me saying 'please do not sign any papers, Carol don't sign the papers' and he was waving his hand around. When I looked up 'papers' in my book it said that it could either be a release from current worries or an involvement in legal matters. When I looked up 'hand', that came up as business too. He'd got a towel at the side of him and a big black umbrella with a huge duck's head on it. In my book that also showed as a connection with business, but in a favourable way. Then, as happens in dreams, I was suddenly somewhere else. I was now in a hospital ward, in the fourth bed along, and according to my book, counting beds is a warning of imminent damage, of being overwhelmed by a load you are carrying on your own.

It was my head I was worried about. My girls told me not to be stupid, that I was born with it so it wouldn't go away But I really felt Spirit was trying to tell me something. So I cancelled my Covid jab for another day. But when I did have it I was really ill for a long time and I remembered the time I'd come face-to-face with myself in bed that night. I looked just like I had looked then.

I suffered for weeks after I'd had my covid jab, making lots of visits to the doctor. Eventually a hospital appointment was made for me. A large lump had appeared on the side of my face which needed investigation. I became very worried.

Prior to my hospital appointment we had a short break in Cannock Chase, at the Silver Tree Holiday Park in Rugeley. We were given the cottage on the site.

It was a beautiful cottage. Absolutely spectacular and the weather was lovely too.

When we opened the front door of the cottage I immediately felt a coldness in the place. Then Steve thought he saw something standing on the stairs. I felt there was more than one, but all I could see was one man on the staircase. I had this feeling he thought I was invading his house so went upstairs to talk to spirit.

"Look, I'm not here to wreck your cottage or anything like that," I said. "I'll treat it with the greatest respect. This is your home and I'm also here to treat you with the greatest respect too."

After that they just left us alone and the whole atmosphere changed. Even Steve commented on how warm it became.

On our last night it was a beautiful evening. We were sitting in the garden and I sat pondering about my forthcoming hospital appointment. Whether I was going to have my face cut for a biopsy. So was feeling a bit down.

I've never asked spirit for anything but I sat there and I just said –

"Right you guys, I do everything for you. I don't want money, I don't want a big win on the lottery and all the rest of it. I just want to know I'm going to be all right tomorrow. I just want to know they're not going to be hacking into my face because that's my nightmare."

Steve said "What sort of signs do you want?"

I didn't really know but then I looked up and all I could see was a big red ball of sunset. So I said "I'd like three stars."

Steve said "Carol you're not going to get three stars, the sunset is too vivid."

As we sat there and it started getting dusk Steve said "Oh that's a big plane" and pointed up to the sky. But then he added "Oh my God it's a star!" Then he looked and spotted another one. And then, lo and behold, for about ten minutes there were three stars twinkling in the sky. Then, as quickly as they had appeared, they disappeared.

The following morning I went into the bathroom, which I'd already found a bit spooky, and suddenly the door flew open. All the doors were solid oak with huge handles so I was quite surprised.

"Steve, is that you?," I shouted, more than once.

But there was no answer.

I went back downstairs and Steve asked, "Were you shouting me?"

"Yes," I said. "Did you just come to the bathroom?"

"No," he said.

So I went back up to the bathroom and this time made sure the door was completely shut.

As I was getting into the shower I said "I am going to be all right today aren't I?"

The door just flew open. I laughed and said – "Are you a peeping Tom?"

But my prayers were answered because the next day I was given the all-clear by the cancer specialist.

Regression

Regression is the process of going back through your life and then back to former lives. Sometimes it can just be curiosity, the thought of – 'who was I in a previous life?" But it can also help you mentally and physically. If you have any problems in your present life, sometimes, going through regression, will help you discover why and how to address them. It can also act as a healing tool to release any bad vibes.

I've been regressed on a number of occasions. The first time was many years ago when I was working at Tamworth Spiritual Church and met an amazing man, Ivor James from Oxfordshire, who used to regress people. He was brilliant and regressed me twice. On both occasions he took me back to Tudor times where apparently I was a lady-in-waiting to Anne Boleyn. People say I've got a lot of knowledge about this period and I can answer questions on buildings that I've been to because I know Henry VIII's been there too. I know where he's been and many different things about him and his court.

There was a two year gap between the two regressions and the first one, being the first one, was so interesting. I remember breathing deep and listening to his instructions then I could feel myself going really heavy eyed. A friend was with me so she heard everything I related.

I must have been in a freezing cold room because I kept saying I was really cold. The walls were stone and all grey but were covered in red drapes. There were lots of beautiful colours in the room – claret reds, peacock blues and greens. There were three people in the room and we were all female and all of us had dark hair. All we did all day was sit, talk and do needlework on circular frames.

We were talking about the month of May. May was mentioned a lot. We all had pearl chokers on and wore fancy hats. Mine had pearls all across the front of it. It was like a semi-circle. One of the group was named Mary, another was Cecily. But I also kept saying that 'Anne had a sharp tongue.' She shouted at most things and was very argumentative, but I said that everything she did, she did with perfection. Almost like OCD these days. She quarrelled and always wanted to be right about everything. If either of us said anything she'd talk us down. She was always right.

During my regression we went on to Hever Castle. It was like a big house. There was a beautiful large brown door and I remember a huge flag flying right above it. There were armour-like statues sanding all in a row. The entrance hall was beautiful. It had a wooden roof and there was a falcon on it. There were letters on a table but I couldn't see what they were. The furniture was beautiful. I love my brasses. I've got lots of brass in my kitchen at home and apparently during my regression I spoke of the highly polished brasses. On the table with the letters there was a long silver knife. A lady sat by the letters, almost as if she was guarding them. In another room there was a statue of armour and a sword. I went into fits of laughter saying that he was wearing a skirt. I kept saying there's a man with an iron skirt on.

In the room we ate in there was a beautiful red tapestry right behind where I was sitting and I kept referring to the two white birds. There was a spiral staircase that we had to climb which covered two floors and there were lots and lots of doors. I remember saying there was a man guarding one of the doors. In another room there was a beautiful four poster bed.

Apparently during the regression I spoke French. I've never spoken French in my life! And I actually used the name Lisle – which ironically is my married name.

As I've said, school was not the best days of my life but even then I was very fascinated with anything to do with Henry VIII, the Tudors, buildings, anything. I did a project at school on this and got really high marks. So it seems that even before I was regressed my past life was there with me.

But now I can relate to things even much more than before. Things that were in the castle, in the rooms, and what was going on outside. When my eldest daughter, Gemma, had to do a history project and asked me to help, I immediately said "Can we do Henry VIII." So we did and I loved it. When it was all finished she got A*** but we were called into the school and questioned – "How did you know this Gemma because it's not in the history books."

All Gemma could say was "but my mum knew."

Her teachers were fascinated because there were things in there from history that they were going to look into – things and places that I'd picked up on. When they delved deeper a lot of what I had said was confirmed and they were intrigued that I knew of places Henry VIII had been.

Again all Gemma could say was, "mum just knows."

We've been places and I've said to Steve "Oh Henry VIII's been here" and he says "Oh what makes you think that?"

Then we've asked questions and they've said "Well yes he has."

I felt it too in Ruthin Castle.

For years I kept saying to Steve "I'm sure Henry VIII was part of this."

Steve would say, "Well it's Wales, so I doubt it."

But there is a massive portrait of Henry VIII on one of the staircases. When I asked why it was there they said "Because he stayed here."

So now even more so, anything to do with Anne Boleyn and the Tudor reign, is just me. When I've been to events where we have to dress up in costume, I always get myself an Anne Boleyn outfit because I'm absolutely fascinated with that woman.

Some years later I was regressed for a third time but this was more traumatic. A friend had just qualified and as I was eager to go through another regression she didn't hesitate to invite me over. I sat back in the chair and listened to Jo's voice telling me to close my eyes and take deep breaths in and out. Her voice floated in my head telling me I would become more relaxed than I had ever been. She told me to visualise a beautiful beach where the sky was a beautiful blue with just a few white fluffy clouds and the sound of the ocean in the background. I was told to relax individual parts of my body. First my forehead, then my eyes and to allow my eyelids to become heavy. To relax my facial muscles, then the back of my neck and around my shoulders, down my back and the curve of my spine. To relax deeper and deeper, my legs, my feet, my toes. I was told to imagine being at the top of some stairs and then she counted me down one by one before telling me I'd reached a corridor through which I was going to float back in time and through the thin veil at the end of the corridor.

I was now in a past life and I began to feel burning.

I was calling out "stop the burning, it's not fair. I've done nothing wrong."

There were lots of people around me and I could see trees and a big hill. I was called Elizabeth and was in my 20's but I didn't know the year. I was wearing a black dress and people were shouting "burn the witch." The women were wearing white hats, they were horrible women, and the men were in dark clothes.

"I'm all tied up," I said. "And I can't breathe."

I could smell burning flesh and I'm sure there were others being burnt too but I didn't know who they were. Then everyone had left and I wasn't burning any more and it was all light, but I could see lots of red.

I knew I'd done nothing wrong, that I had just wanted to help people. I'd been helping a lady who was ill and had made her soup from fresh vegetables in a little terracotta bowl. She lived near me but was all alone. I lived with my father who I had a good relationship with but my mother was dead. She had also been burned as a witch. I'd had a brother called Andrew but he had died young through illness. My father had tried to stop them but the men had come and taken me.

"They don't listen," I said. "It's no good talking to them."

It was quite an experience but hardly surprising considering my love of all things 'witchy'.

I went back to Jo a couple of weeks later and took Steve with me but unfortunately he proved to be the type who can't regress. There are a few people like this, their present day psyche blocks their past life's psyche. Once again though I went quickly back.

My name this time was Grace Jones and I had died in 1879. I had a big house and I explained that as I walked in, there were numerous paintings in gold and gilt frames. They were proper paintings and they were everywhere. There was a dining table which was huge, it must have had 16 or 20 chairs around it. I was sorting the cutlery out so Jo asked me if I was a maid.

"No," I said. "This is my house."

I said I was married to someone who was very rich and lived in what I kept describing as a big Georgian mansion house in Surrey with loads of windows. I was wearing a long green dress with a big cream collar. It was very splendid. In the room with me was my husband, who was called Charles, and my son called James, who was aged four. But I kept saying – "He's a nasty man, he's a nasty man," and I got very emotional with tears running down my face.

I said that he was always making me cry, that he was spiteful.

"He's horrid to me, he treats me awful," I said.

Then we went on a bit further and I was lying in a large four poster bed and my son was grown up. I wasn't old, but I wasn't young either. My husband had died by now. There was a doctor standing by me and I was screaming because it was the same doctor who had performed my first bowel operation in 1997 which had gone wrong.

I was screaming, "He's cut me, he's cut me down there, and he's killed me."

The next thing I was looking at my grave so Jo asked me where I was being buried.

"Surrey," I said. It was a great big grave with Grace Jones written on the stone.

Jo then asked me where I'd like to go now and I said Wales.

"In two years time I'll be living in Wales," I said.

At this point Jo felt I'd skipped regression and come back into my present life. She asked if I'd be happy leaving my house and I said, "Yes."

"So are you happy in your house at the moment," she asked.

"No," I said. "I'm happy when I go to Wales, that's my life now."

The splendours of Ruthin Castle

The splendours of Ruthin Castle

Our bedroom in Ruthin Castle

That same bedroom plus sword

Feeling happy in Ruthin Castle

The little girl in the photograph. Is it really me?

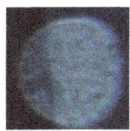
A face in the wall in Pendle.
Is it one of the witches?

Orbs of protection in Chatsworth House

Paranormal investigations

Sometimes I go into places and people say "oh it's horrible" but to me it just feels so lovely. I always say – "The dead won't hurt you, it's the living that hurt you."

I've experienced lots of weird things but I always remember the pact I have had with spirit since I was a little girl. That I will treat them with respect however badly some of them are acting. Even when cupboard doors are flying open and things are being thrown about.

I have spent many evenings in my home town of Tamworth.

We did Rage, the hairdressers in Tamworth, which is up an alleyway amongst other small shops. They're all old buildings and behind is a courtyard where they used to keep all the horses which would carry smuggled goods, and bodies, to the Moat House. One of the girls who worked there said she would put nail varnishes down and they'd either be missing the next day or they'd be all over the floor. The owner of Rage at the time was a non-believer and was cracking jokes, but when one of the trolleys flew across the floor I think he changed his mind.

"Oh Carol," he said. "I won't take the mickey any more."

A short while later we were sitting looking out of the window at all the normal Saturday night crowds and suddenly all the lights went on upstairs.

But that whole area is alive with spirit. Another place I did in that row, which was a beautician's, who had had complaints from customers who found the place so cold. On the night I was there, there was lots of noise and banging, and again items were strewn on the floor. I think the buildings are all connected. I think that perhaps they were all one building at one time and spirit belongs to that one building and now goes around all these newer, smaller premises thinking they're still just in one building. Spirits do often live in their own times.

Another time I was asked to visit the Manor House in Tamworth. An old beautiful house which was, and still is, being used as a day care centre for the elderly, and where they were having strange things happening. Things kept going missing. The person who ran it would put a pan down in the kitchen, turn round and it was gone. Although I did feel lots of things there, there was nothing sinister. I could see people who had passed on but who still wanted to visit for the company. There was just happiness everywhere. However when I was sitting chatting to the people who came there for the company the place offered, I looked up at a mirror and there was the image of a dog. It was just a plain wall opposite so nothing could have been reflected across from there.

Sometimes I worked alone, sometimes with a friend called Tracey. On one occasion we went to a house in Birmingham where the woman there had noticed that whenever she cleaned her hairbrush and threw the tufts of hair into the bin, they had later disappeared. She also had a sensation of being raped. In one of the rooms there was a huge portrait of a man with gilt all around the frame. It was a proper oil painting. When we were looking around we saw it in the bedroom but when we went back into the room, after walking around the house, it wasn't there. After searching we found it had been moved to another room. It was a mystery as we had all been downstairs, nobody was upstairs, so who could have moved it?

One night we were faced with quite a malevolent spirit, who luckily I was able to calm down. The house was quite close to where I live and the owner got in touch saying she'd moved up here from down south, with her husband and two girls, and needed me to go and cleanse her house. She said the girls were being threatened in their bedrooms. One had been thrown across the room at one point.

Without a doubt there was an entity upstairs and it took a couple of visits until the place was calm again. On one visit Tracey sat at the dining room table and I sat in the living room. It was unusual because all the furniture had been left in the house belonging to the previous occupants. Normally the vendors take the furniture with them and the purchasers bring there own, but this wasn't the case here. So I was sitting on an old couch that had belonged to the previous family. All of a sudden this gentleman started talking to me. He explained that his wife had had an affair with the man over the road and then he'd got cancer and was dying. His wife hadn't cared about him so when he died he decided to take over the house.

He was the type of spirit who felt that it was his house and no one was going to get in. So when the young couple came with their children he was trying to brainwash the girls. The mother did research the story, and even met the wife, so discovered the story was completely true. After he had had his chat with me he disappeared. Then I saw the children later at a party and they thanked me saying "We don't have that man come and talk to us any more."

I came across another spirit who didn't want a family living in his house. A friend of mine, Laura, had asked me to cleanse her house. She was having things moved. So I went. It was an old rented property in Tamworth and when I went into her little boy Charlie's room there was a man standing there. He was called George and said he felt as if his house was being taken over. He told me to go away and that he would not share his house with this family. I was told to get out and take the family with me.

"No!" I said, "You've got to stop being selfish and share this house."

This did seem to calm him down. He even went on to tell me where he was buried in the local cemetery on the Glascote Road. Laura took me over there and I didn't have to search for the grave. I just went straight to it.

I went to a beauty rooms in Tamworth once. They had advertised on Facebook that they wanted someone to help as they'd had all sorts of weird things happening. Although they did have someone offer to help, as I actually did the cards for one of the girls there, she phoned me to see if I could help. So I went along.

Laura asked if I could first just have a walk around and see what I felt. It was a huge building on an industrial estate in Amington, which was once a coal mining area, and she had done some research into the history of the place. I went into the little office and picked up a couple of things in there and then walked upstairs. As soon as I got up the stairs I felt someone was hanging or choking. Laura then told me that the boyfriend of one of the girls who worked there had just hung himself.

I went into another room.

"Please be careful." I said. "There are two things. Number one, you have someone working for you who is basically two-faced. I don't want to lose anyone their job, but unless you get rid of that person you're going to be pulled right down. Secondly, we need to calm a few things down in here. Or you're going to lose all your machines."

So she asked me if I, together with her friend who does the stones, would go in and do a thorough cleansing. I agreed and we went over one day when the facility was closed so we could have the place to ourselves. After the visit things did calm down and there were no problems after that.

When I had been in the beauty rooms I'd seen an iron door.

"Can I go in there?" I asked.

When I opened the door it was like being in an old prison. No windows, the paintwork going, it was all very dank and dark. As I went further into the corridor I began reeling off all these names. I didn't know where they were coming from but my head was full of them. There was a Bill Hammond, a Sam Day who was a driver, someone called Ann who had lost a child down there and many more.

"You've just blown me away," Laura said. "You've just named nine of the people who were killed down here in the old pit."

One was trampled to death by the horses. One fell down and drowned. Another one was run over. Most of them were only young lads but they were all talking to me at once so I couldn't pick everything up.

The owner did come to see me later and I immediately picked up on another problem. She needed to be careful because money was going missing so suggested she put some camera's up. Which she did. They caught the person doing it and once again everything calmed down.

Often when I do a paranormal investigation there may be someone who doesn't take the event seriously. They want me to get spirit to do something horrific, like in the movies, such as throw things but I always say –

"They're not performing seals. They don't just jump to order."

I will never ask them to do anything like that because I think it is disrespectful. But it can be helpful to use a caller and then I can stay in the background and provide the energy. A caller is someone who asks them to come, whereas I just wait for them to come to me. On occasions I have felt the presence entering the room and then discovered the caller has gone into a trance.

A lot of people get satisfaction from meditation but I'm afraid I don't, so I never liked being part of that circle. Certainly where requests were made to move things. People say to me how can you get away without asking for things to be moved. Admittedly I have been in situations where I've sat there and nothing has happened. But if I'm patient and spirit can see I'm being respectful, things usually start to happen. I have been in tricky situations where nothing has happened. We've sat there waiting and waiting and then I just say –

"Right. Ok. They don't want to talk to me today," and I've just walked away.

But that has only happened occasionally. Ninety per cent of the time things do happen.

Other times I've been to places where they've put toys or other items on the floor, hoping they'll be moved, or scattered sand or flour around to see if any marks are left behind. Sometimes it can be just a ripple, like a small wave or the wind has shifted it. Often if an item was moved I always felt that spirit was quite happy to take part in a little game. But nowadays they use machines and monitors which can pick up sounds, even voices sometimes.

I've been asked to do all sorts and I've also been with people who are very aggressive. Those times I have thought –

"Oh if I was you. I'd watch what you were doing because you might get a knife thrown at you or something.'

So you do have to be careful and experienced in what you do.

Sometimes someone will come into my kitchen and say –

"Go on then ask them my name," and I say "sorry you're with the wrong medium."

They either give me the names or they don't. I do what spirit tells me to do. And even though I'm doing a service I forget that person is in the room and I do it for spirit world. But I've never, ever, shouted out or asked them to do this, do that, or do the other.

I once attended the program Most Haunted when we were at Ruthin Castle in Wales. We were sitting in the Medieval Banqueting Hall and I got very emotional because I could see a lady a short distance away. For the first time I went into a trance. All of a sudden I just looked up and there she was, the Lady Grey, and I started to cry. Steve looked at me, I don't actually recall it, but I was apparently sobbing. Steve was shouting for them to stop filming so he could get me out, but no one could hear him. The same as what had happened to me in the past. Then a young make-up artist happened to look at me and screamed, just as a large Welsh wooden spoon flew through the air and landed on the table by them.

Some years ago I worked with Caroline Martin and Deano on The Sanctuary, a radio show which went out live on Sunday nights, on BRMB radio. One Sunday evening we visited Dudley Castle. Built in the eleventh century, its very much a ruin now. A Royalist stronghold during the civil war it went on to become an important part of the Black Country at the start of the Industrial Revolution. Coal mines and quarries were cut deep below the castle and many men lost their lives in the network of tunnels.

We went up into the tower at the start of our investigation but I couldn't feel too much there so we went out into the ruins. It was now that I started to hear a loud noise. I didn't think anyone else could hear it but then Steve said to me – "Did you hear that?" It was like a loud clucking sound.

"Well if you're hearing it, why isn't anyone else?" I asked.

But then Deano said he heard something.

Of course for the radio program Caroline was thinking that this was going to be good, but I felt we needed to make a move and fast. I didn't know what it was but I knew it wasn't good and that we needed to run. So we did, live on air. All we could hear was this horrendous screeching behind us, something like I'd never heard before, and all the doors were shaking.

Later when we listened back to the recording I realised it was the well-known Phoenix, a half-witch, half-bird creature of the spirit world which resembles a huge horrible looking bird. The old ruins in Dudley Castle were used years ago as kitchens where the witches made all their potions and that night they'd been called up.

Afterwards we left to go to a nearby cottage and were being led there by a warden. But I didn't want to go the way he was directing us.

"Why don't you want to go this way," he said. "Ninety percent of mediums always want to go this way."

"Because I feel this is the way I want to go," I said.

So he agreed. Then at a certain point I stopped and said "There's a tunnel here."

He smiled and said "She's dead right and no other medium has ever found it."

The tunnel actually goes down into Dudley Castle. It's probably where they took bodies years and years ago because I could feel such a lot of activity down there.

We now made our way to an old derelict cottage on the estate. In this cottage there's supposed to be a mad man. The axe man they call him. When we arrived at the cottage I could see a little girl in the window with long dark hair. But because the structure was unsafe I wasn't allowed in which was unfortunate because I felt there was such a lot of activity in there.

That was one of my best nights but I was so ill afterwards. I didn't get up for three days. It was like they had hexed me and given me a curse. Sometimes I am asked if I have ever come across bad spirits and it is always that phoenix at Dudley Castle that comes to mind.

The Station Hotel in Dudley is really haunted. Dating back to 1898 it is a black and white building with a courtyard and old stable building, with the main entrance for horses and carriages being on the Trindle and Castle Hill. It has been modernised and extended twice. Once in 1936 and then again in the 1960's. In its heyday it would have been described as an upper class, modern hotel. I was asked to go there by a friend to show a group of people around. I took my friend Tracey with me, and Steve came along too. The place is fantastic, but there is quite a nasty spirit in the hotel who caused one person to actually start going into a trance. This did worry me because you've got to know how to get them out. The young man was sitting in a chair on one side of the room and I could see him gradually going off and beginning to transfigure from a man to a woman.

"Get him out of here." I was yelling. "Get him out!"

It was in room 214 and he wasn't the first person I've heard of going into a trance in that room. In the corner, opposite where he was sitting there was a rocking chair which was moving. Apparently someone had died while sitting in that rocking chair.

There are lots of poltergeist activities in that hotel. Things flying around and lots of different lights and orbs. The staircase is typical of old grand hotels and as we stood at the top looking down we could see all the activity happening. In the courtyard we could hear children and horses.

"I can feel that children have died here on the cobbles," I said. "While they were playing, the horses were coming in and out."

We went into the cellar and I kept mentioning a chute. Apparently one of the owners tried to have his wicked way with a young servant but she fought him off. When she threatened to tell his wife he killed her and put her in a barrel then tossed her down the chute used for the barrels.

Standing outside the front of the hotel, which faces Dudley Castle, I kept saying "She's buried there. She's buried there."

Guy's Cliff House in Warwick was an old Gothic mansion which has been destroyed by fire. It was built in 1751 by Samuel Greatheed, the member of parliament for Coventry. During WW1 it was a hospital and during the second world war, a school for evacuated children. In the 1950's it was bought with the intention of turning it into a hotel. But this didn't happen and it was left to decay. In 1992 it was used to film a scene for the television series, The Adventures of Sherlock Holmes, which involved a fire. The fire got out of control and the house was badly damaged.

I did this investigation when I worked with Caroline Martin on The Santuary. There was one medium in the stables and I was underground in a sort-of bunker, cellar type-place. I'm not very good in confined spaces but there were only a couple of steps down into it and then there was plenty of room to stand up, so I was quite happy with that.

As soon as we walked in I could immediately sense there was a lot of poltergeist activity. We were sitting on long bench-like chairs which were scattered about the floor, and I could feel things flying around us. At one point papers, which were on a shelf on the nearby wall, suddenly just flew through the air in front of us. There was a lot of noise, like dragging sounds, and there were coloured orbs. You could hear the sounds of people and horses walking above us. When we put the lights on they would go off and then come on again then off again, repeatedly. That's the energy you see once again causing modern technology to react in a strange way.

Myself and the other medium changed places and I went into the stables but there wasn't a lot of energy there. In fact after what I had experienced in the cellar I got quite bored in the stables. But we both had roughly the same experiences as each other, with all the activity being in the cellar. Although we couldn't go into the house, as it is in ruins since it was burnt down, our investigations continued until 4 o'clock in the morning. We explored all the outbuildings and were able to go into one of the rooms of the old house, but it was the cellar that did it for me, there was so much activity down there.

Another of my favourite places was the Moat House in Tamworth. It was built in 1572 by William Harcourt who was married to the daughter of a wealthy Tamworth family – the Comberfords – and when the couple died the house was passed through the family until they were forced to sell it during the Civil War. Afterwards it passed through many owners. I know they used to hang witches there and I've found graves that no one knew about. I've often seen a lady floating towards me.

There were two rooms in particular where I could feel most of the activity and it was in these two rooms that I was scared people had been killed years ago. I was told that this was true and their body parts had been taken away to be used for medical research and suchlike. And if somebody wanted something on the black market, a tooth, or a kidney, or an eye, that's where they used to do it. In the late 1800's it was also used as a private nursing home for the mentally ill.

People have had strange experiences in both the toilets and the kitchens so when it was being sold myself and my friend Tracey were given the keys to have a look around while it was being stripped down. As we walked into the kitchen we had a knife thrown at us.

Tracey laughed. "Yes we're here," she said. "But we're not here to hurt you"

"And you can stop that now." I added. "I'm here and this is the last time I'll be coming. We just want to say goodbye to you."

Then the whole atmosphere changed and it was lovely.

We had so many memories of other visits there. Once we found a monk's grave there, that no one knew about, and there were old tunnels used by the monks to escape. And for the nuns to visit the monks in secret. Another time we went into the library. There's an old oven built into a large fireplace. It was here they hung the witches and the hook was still there. As I stood by the fire place I felt I was being strangled.

Steve looked at me and asked what was wrong.

"I don't know," I said "but I feel I'm choking.

Then I moved back and somebody showed me where the hook was.

I found priest holes there too. Just by the kitchen there's a solid wall and I kept saying there's a hole in there. I not only felt a presence in them, but I could feel the wealth of that being too. I kept getting told no, there was nothing there, but when the place was refurbished they found it. There are tunnels there too which go straight through to Tamworth Castle. That place had more history than anywhere else but the new owners have now had it cleansed.

I once held an event there, with the help of friends, to raise money for Behcet's Syndrome which my daughter suffers from. We charged £10 a ticket and had acquired loads of raffle prizes from various outlets in the area – free haircuts, free nail treatments, fish and chip suppers, crates of wine, bottles of spirits, a night in a hotel, tickets for the Tamworth Snow Dome arena and many more. We had five separate tables scattered around the room for people to sit and I moved among them giving readings. My lovely friend Sue from the Cottage Healing Centre in Tamworth, was doing Indian massage in one area and another friend, Laura, who is a holistic healer, did the stones. She'd give people the stones to feel and then tell them what she got about the person and such-like. Then there were two other people reading tarot cards and angel cards and someone doing reiki healing. So there were things going on the whole of the time.

We had a buffet and then at the end of the night I, after a health and safety demonstration, took everybody on a tour of the Moat House. People still talk about it today. How they saw the white lady coming down and how one of the girls, who is a non-believer, actually felt she was being pushed and then saw a woman coming towards her.

I would love to start doing paranormal investigations again. It was always such a lovely experience. The group meet up and get ready to go, mainly getting all the equipment ready. We had all the proper equipment, electricity lines, white noise, all sorts. What stops people doing these investigations now is the cost of the liability insurance, in case anyone falls. Sometimes you have to take out a cover for up to a million pounds so the premiums can be really high and costly. When I did the Moat House I had to take out two million pounds worth of insurance because if anyone fell, or whatever, I had to have all the correct cover. That is why a lot of the paranormal teams have folded now. It's too costly for what they can charge the public. At one time you could go on one of these investigations for less than £10 but not any more. They were lovely times.

Spirits in the night

I once worked with a lovely group who called themselves Spirits in the Night. We used to put markers out. We'd sprinkle flour or talcum powder, or put an object like old coins, crosses, teddy bears and at various times we've had those things moved. We would split up into little groups and then come together at the end to compare what had happened and more often than not, mine would be double to what anyone else had experienced. Usually there was a caller, Sheryl mainly did that, and I provided the energy to attract spirit.

While working with Spirits of the Night I witnessed many unusual happenings which involved other members of the group. One in particular happened one night at Tutbury Castle.

Built after the Norman invasion this castle was given to Henry de Ferrers, a powerful Norman lord, and remained with that family until 1266. Following the Baron's Wars it was confiscated and given to Edmund Crouchback, Earl of Lancaster. Destroyed by parliamentary forces during the Civil War much of it has remained a ruin ever since. Mary, Queen of Scots, was held prisoner there and Henry VIII also visited the castle. But our visit proved quite exceptional.

At first we went into one of the outbuildings. It was a large building with no roof on it and there were lots of pigeons roosting in it. I don't know what it was originally used for, although we did notice an old metal oven-housing on one side.

Joy, one of our members, is quite susceptible, although she can't pick up names and things she can be very susceptible and affected by her surroundings. We were walking around and as normal it was freezing cold. All of a sudden she started shaking her hand. In fact she couldn't stop it from flapping. Then her glove fell off and as soon as that happened her hand stopped moving. As it did she felt someone take hold of her hand. All the time we walked around she could feel a small hand holding hers. But her hand got cold again, so she put her glove back on and as soon as she did her hand started flapping again. Then as soon as the glove came off it would stop and she would feel someone holding her hand. By now she had became very emotional.

Later we went off into the actual castle, the part which isn't a ruin, and went up into what is known as the King's Room. In that room there was a throne-like chair and in the middle of the room there was a staircase going down with balustrades round it. While in the room Joy and her sister Ann were sitting together and Sheryl was calling out asking if there was anybody there – "If there are any spirits please come forward." Then Joy started to get emotional again. She was rocking in her seat, getting faster and faster. Then, as she made crying noises, she lifted her hands as if to protect her face. It was like she was defending herself because she was being hit. Then she started crying and screaming. She was becoming more and more distressed so Sheryl took over.

"The spirit which is in you now, please leave." Sheryl called out. "Please leave Joy alone. Get out of her body."

In that instance we saw a light shoot out of her chest and she collapsed down into her chair. Two of the men picked her up and carried her out. She was exhausted and her body was just limp. We all felt it was now time for a break, so looked for somewhere to rest and enjoy the food and drinks we always took with us. Afterwards we left Joy with her sister to calm down while we went off to investigate other parts.

Later we went back into the King's Room and it seems that because Joy wasn't with us there was nothing to pick up. The night seemed to be centred around Joy. We had now picked up that it was a little girl holding her hand and who was trying to lead her somewhere. And that it was also the little girl who was being hit.

We then went downstairs and into a longish room, where we all sat around on the chairs in various parts of this room. The guard from Tutbury was standing by the far wall watching us. Joy and Annie were sitting under the stairs. And another of our members, Ian, was standing at the top of the stairs looking down. He told us he felt very cold and other people said they were picking up something on the stairs. I could feel that someone was up there watching us. It was like someone was peering over the bannister. And it was that person who had killed the little girl. He had worked for the king and from what we picked up we think she was an illegitimate child of somebody quite high up so she had to go. She was about four or five years old. Joy, who was sitting underneath, began rocking while humming a childish tune. Then we were all singing 'ring-a-ring-a-roses'. A song which dates back to the Great Plague in 1665 so the little girl could have belonged to a period anytime after that.

Then Joy got emotional again and she was crying and crying. Once again we asked the little girl to go in peace and rest. This time she did but as she left, the one which was upstairs, moved. Ian didn't feel anyone touching him but he felt somebody was there, close to him, and he was cold. The guard couldn't believe what was happening and on the strength of what he relayed back to the owners we were asked back a second time. Unfortunately I couldn't go on the second investigation, and Joy didn't go either. I heard later from Sheryl that on that occasion nothing was picked up.

Another paranormal investigation I did with Spirits in the Night was at the Hawkesyard Estate in Rugeley. Again another historic place which dates back to 1337 when the original hall had been built by Simon de Rugeley. Three hundred years later it was just a ruin and lay derelict until 1759 when the estate was bought by Nathaniel Lister, a poet and writer. He married a Lichfield heiress, Martha Fletcher, and built a new mansion house on the site. Eighty years later it was bought by Mary Spode, of the pottery family, as a present for her son, Josiah IV, and more alterations took place. When Josiah died in 1893 the estate was inherited by his niece, Helen Gulson. After a 'vision' she built a priory there in 1898. Occupied at first by nuns it later became a monastery which closed in 1988.

On our investigations Sheryl was once again the caller but nothing seemed to be happening, so I went off walking on my own. I went into the room in which I think they marry people now to have a look around. There had already been two mediums in this room, which as I've said is how they worked – different mediums in different rooms just to see if the same story came up. When nothing happened I just sat there and to be honest I was bored. But some nights I did get bored if things were quiet.

However it didn't stay quiet for long. Suddenly the door slammed and I felt someone right behind me, almost breathing down my neck. So I started talking, the usual stuff like – oh hello, are you here to talk to me and such-like, but nothing happened. So I left and headed out into the gardens. Steve had come with me and had been taking photographs and as we walked away he said he felt we were being followed. He was right. We were being followed. And by what felt like a huge dog. Steve took some more photographs and in them you could see the animal's eyes.

We then found ourselves outside the priory. It looked as if nobody was in there but all the lights were on. We went in and while there I saw two monks and a nun. And the only way I can describe it, is that they were up to no good.

Standing outside I suddenly started calling, "Helen, Helen."

I didn't know who Helen was then but later heard the story of the owner, Helen Gulson, going out into the garden one day and seeing the vision of Mary Magdalene. And that after experiencing this she had decided to build the abbey on that very spot.

From there we went into the monk's cemetery. It was all overgrown so we had to be careful where we were walking. The cemetery was filled with stone crosses and underneath are lots of tunnels. There were lots of orbs and lights and I could see a whole row of stone crosses were all dated 1952. It turned out there had been a flu epidemic that year and many of the monks had died.

As I got down on my hands and knees and started rubbing the inscriptions all the orbs and lights kept flashing around me.

We went back to meet up with the group and Steve told them what we had experienced. The other two mediums got together but the only thing that came up the same, was that one medium said when she was in the room where the weddings took place, she also felt she was being watched.

It is known from the history of the place that they did used to sneak the 'naughty' nuns in to visit the monks. And of course Rugeley is very close to Cannock Chase where there used to be a story of a big black cat roaming the chase. So they thought it was the black cat we'd picked up that night. But it is also said that somebody had died in that room years ago.

The first investigation I did with Spirits of the Night was a house in Tamworth. There was a spirit there called George and what had been happening, was all down to the fact they'd been using a Ouija Board, which I hate. While using it they had opened a vortex. It was awful. Crucifixes were hanging upside down and the woman claimed that George had raped her on a couple of occasions.

I had no idea who this George was but he was obviously something to do with the occult because he was dark and demonic. Certainly something too hot to handle and there wasn't anything we could do. They had to call a priest in. But while we were there I did pick something up. We were sitting in the little girl's bedroom and I could suddenly smell burning, although no one else could. Three weeks later all the bedrooms in the house caught fire. This story did eventually appear in the News of the World newspaper – a woman being raped by spirit.

A very special place is Grace Dieu Priory which is on the Loughborough to Ashby-de-la-Zouch road in Leicestershire. It was built between 1235 and 1241 and also housed a small hospital. After it was dissolved in 1538 it was taken over by the Beaumont family who built a house there. The property was held by descendants of the Beaumont's until the late seventeenth century when it was partly demolished and left as a ruin. The ruins of the old priory are also still there.

We were met in the car park by a lady with torches who told us to be careful, as it could be difficult underfoot.

"You won't cover it all in one night," she said.

But as normal there was a big group of us so we split into two smaller groups. It was freezing that night, we were wrapped up in scarves, hats, coats, everything, but we all had experiences of going hot and cold.

It was a big massive woodland area, the type of area which could be really difficult when you were out there at night. You could get all sorts of other noises too, animals and such-like, so had to listen very carefully to pick anything up. But we did hear noises, really strange noises, and we had the constant feeling we were being followed. It was absolutely pitch black but we could see lights in the trees. I could also feel that hangings had taken place amongst the trees. I had the sensation of people staring out of the darkness at us. At one point we thought we were being followed because we could hear footsteps behind us. You could actually hear the clipping of heels but when you turned round there was nobody there. I felt babies had been buried there too, and dogs.

We were also followed by a dog. We knew it was there but we couldn't see it.

Some of us went up onto the viaduct while some stayed underneath and we got really strange sensations there. Weird things, like feeling we were being followed or being pushed. When I was up on the viaduct I could feel people rushing past us. When the two groups swapped over we all experienced the same things and had the same feelings. The strongest of all was that we all saw Roman soldiers marching across the nearby fields.

There were three stone buildings to explore. The largest one being the Priory, but one of the smaller ones in particular really freaked me. It was very weird and I kept saying to Steve that I felt like we were being watched.

Then we wandered over the surrounding fields and before we knew it we were back where we had started, although we'd walked for ages. Every time we split up into our groups, we ended up meeting again, and it seemed like we were just going around in constant circles. We didn't know where we were and it was so black but we were all laughing and joking about it. We always had a laugh on these occasions.

Then there was a light. It was about 2 o'clock in the morning and we were walking down a path trying to get back to our cars. It was dark and we were discussing which way to go when suddenly a big light appeared. We looked over to where it was but there was nobody there, nobody at all. It then appeared to lead us back to where we wanted to be and once we were back it disappeared.

Grace Dieu is a huge place but despite what we were told at the beginning I think we did cover all of it.

It was a really good night. Quite an emotional night because one minute you were up, the next you were down. I hadn't been looking forward to it, being outside all the time, but the lights made it so fascinating. I also had sensed there had been a canal there, which had been filled in. They had tried to open it up at some point and then filled it in again. I could certainly feel the existence of water and that there had been drownings. We usually did our investigations before being told any history so sensing drownings surprised me. It wasn't until later that I found out there had been a canal there.

Canals, of course, can be very interesting places. We once went to Atherstone Locks and the adjoining Lock Keepers Cottage on the Coventry Canal. Although it was a short night it proved to be an interesting night. We included all the outer buildings but some weren't that good so we had finished by half one. The Lock Keeper's Cottage is quite an old house with cellars. Years ago all the contraband brought up the canal was hidden in these cellars. But I also felt evidence of some tunnels. I love the presence of tunnels. There is always so much activity in them.

Behind one of the walls I kept saying – "There's a tunnel, there's a tunnel."

Later when the owner was having some work done he phoned Sheryl to tell her I was right, they had found a tunnel.

We'd been called in because the owner, Tony, kept waking up and feeling something on his face. He was feeling that someone was trying to suffocate him. My feelings told me that spirit was actually sitting on him while he was in bed. Tony was quite a sceptical man so wasn't really believing what was happening but I walked in and immediately saw a dog.

I said "you've just put a collar away in a drawer," and his wife got quite emotional.

When I went into the bedroom I saw the dog sitting by the bed. I described the dog and he said "do you know that's really comforted me."

They had only recently lost their dog.

Their cooker used to rattle and make a noise as if it was being scraped across the floor. Where it was standing, years and years before, there had been a door. Spirits were still using the old doorway because to them, in their time, it was still a doorway and the vibration from the door being opened was causing the cooker to vibrate.

A lady in our group was sitting on a chair and suddenly started becoming breathless. It appeared that spirit was sitting on her, like it did the owner, so we quickly got her out of the house. Then another of our party, who was upstairs, suddenly came rushing downstairs and ran out of the house as if he was chasing somebody. But once outside it had quickly disappeared.

The spirit was a very disturbed one and was making Tony so emotional he would cry. He felt like he was being "got at" and then developed panic attacks. We asked it to go, well Sheryl as the caller asked it to go, and things did calm down after that. But it was a very powerful spirit.

This spirit also used to walk the locks. Of course you're not supposed to walk the locks at night and this was two o'clock in the morning but we'd had permission from the Waterways to be there so me and Steve, with Sheryl behind, walked along the towpath. We could hear people and horses. People have drowned in those locks and as we were walking along I could feel them. I could feel that one was only a child. When we got back the lock-keeper said yes there had been an incident which involved a child.

But the strongest feeling I had by the canal was that I felt somebody had jumped in while being chased, and died. I just stopped and said 'somebody jumped in and died here.'

"Help him," I was shouting, "He's got to get out."

I felt that three had jumped in and were trying to get to the other side and that they were trying to get away from other people. The one who had died was a young man in his twenties. He had swum over but when he had tried to get out the other side he couldn't. He'd misjudged the bank and discovered there was a wall in his way. He'd banged his head then hadn't got the strength to get further down where there was an opening. My feeling was that it had happened quite recent to our visit.

When we went back and was talking to Tony he couldn't believe it because it had happened within the previous ten years. It concerned some men who had been involved in robberies in the area and had run down off the main road, the Coleshill Road, onto the canal tow path. The police were chasing them and one had jumped in, thinking he could get over to the other side, but he'd swam at the wall in the darkness and had drowned. The police had dragged him out and tried to resuscitate him but it was too late. His mates however, hadn't stuck around.

Hartshill is also part of the British Waterways and we went there on another occasion. It contains outbuildings, which include a worker's house and repair yards for boats. We did the outbuildings first. David, one of our members, felt he was being targetted by someone who was disfigured. But he had a habit of playing with spirit. If we got a spirit when David was with us he would, depending on what it was or who it was, try to wind it up.

We had picked this spirit up while sitting in one of the workshops. He'd been crushed in some way while he was working in there and had been disfigured, and his spirit still worked in there. The workshop had a door very similar to that of a stable door, the top bit of which was open. Through this gap we could see a sign hanging on the wall just outside. It kept moving. It wasn't windy, it was a very still night, but every time we asked spirit a question, the sign moved.

Outside I picked up that someone had been killed on the road across the bridge. A young lad. He'd been knocked off his motorbike on the Hartshill side of the bridge, by the house. I was getting the sound of the screech of brakes.

We went up into the clock tower. At first nothing happening and Sheryl and I just sat talking. Then, all of a sudden, the place was filled with bats. I don't cope very well with bats, I don't like them and they were flying everywhere, diving, all sorts, so I had to get out. I was panicking because in those days I wore a lot of hair lacquer.

I found the house more interesting than the buildings. There was a white door with little stairs that led down to the cellar. I don't usually like confined spaces but I did manage to get down them and into the cellar. And regardless of my claustrophobia I still felt it was a horrible place. In the house there was a wonderful staircase. But it was also full of porcelain dolls. I probably sound very sensitive but I don't like porcelain dolls either. I don't know why, but I have got a real thing about them. And that house was full of them. Everywhere you went there were these dolls looking at you. Like something out of a horror story.

They were only a young couple who rented the house and they had no children. But I remember going up into a huge bedroom. It was a child's bedroom, like an old fashioned nursery. It had got a massive train track on the floor with little trains and trucks. When we went upstairs for a second time the train had moved and there was water on the floor. But there was nowhere the water could have leaked from. The couple said they could always hear children playing up there. And running. They could hear voices but they weren't loud enough to make out what they saying.

I sat on the bed and had to take my scarf off because I felt really really hot. The children appeared and I started talking to them. There were three of them but I didn't feel that anything untoward had happened to them. All we could hear was giggling, lots of giggling, like children playing. Then we heard footsteps coming up the stairs and thought it was another member of our group. But when Sheryl and I looked, there was no one there.

The couple told us that water was always appearing on the floor. We felt the children were there because they had died at that age. There was no evidence that there'd been a fire, which is why water had been used, so we felt the children had drowned in the canal at the front of the house and brought the water in with them.

Every time we walked down the stairs I felt like someone was behind us. And that there was someone guarding the top of the stairs, perhaps their mother.

The Castle Hotel in Tamworth was the Magistrates Hall years ago, and they used to hang witches in there. Inside is a Jacobean room, called the Oak Room, with all oak panelling and beams. It was from these beams they hung people. The panelling is made of beautiful brown wood but I knew there were tunnels behind this panelling. Sure enough when they were doing some refurbishment later, they did find the tunnels. There was also a little shabby kitchen from where you could see the castle. I was amazed how close the castle appeared from here. You could almost touch it. It appeared just outside the window, but when you went out it looked further away, miles in fact.

It started to feel cold so we went out, but before leaving we left a teddy bear on the floor. When we went back in, it had been turned around and was facing the opposite direction. We had shut the door behind us so nobody could have gone in.

While doing the investigation there I went up to a bedroom right at the top of the hotel. I walked in and thought somebody was smoking. They all laughed.

"But something's burning," I said.

Then I felt sick because I could smell the burning of flesh. I could smell death and feel the burning and the heat. Then they told me about the fire in 1838 and how six maids had perished in that room because they couldn't get out. One maid, Elizabeth, had tried to protect them all and she's now buried in St Editha's, the parish church of Tamworth.

Outside there are some double gates and just at the side, as you go through, there's a drain.

"There's a tunnel there." I said and I was right. It takes you straight into the castle.

In the adjoining courtyard you could hear horses moving around, the clopping of their hooves, and the wheels of the carts.

It was 3 o'clock in the morning when I'd gone outside and I felt exhausted after picking up all that I had, the fire and then all the tunnels leading to the castle. Suddenly this bolt of lightning came and I screamed. Brightening the mood someone jokingly said, "you've just been doing ghost hunting in here and you're scared of a bit of lightning."

Opposite the Castle Hotel is the Brewery. Although called the Brewery it's been many, many things over the years, including the workhouse at one time. So from the hotel we went across there. But it was a dead-end and we didn't get anything in there.

The Colin Grazier Hotel is a very popular venue in Tamworth but is also very haunted. Named after a sailor from Tamworth who was killed in action during World War 2, part of the building was once the police station. We didn't pick anything up in the rooms upstairs so we went down into what would have been the police cells years ago. The area was shaped like a 'V'. Men and boys would have been on the one side and women, girls and children on the other side. It depended on their age which side the boys went.

We felt the presence of one police officer in particular. He came across as a really nasty person who was horrible to both the women and the young children. One of the other mediums was standing opposite me and we were feeding off each other, picking up the same things. David was with us again, and once again was antagonising spirit and asking – "What did you do? What did you do to the little girls? Were you into the men or boys? What did you do to the little boys?" All sorts of questions and then Mark, who was standing opposite me, started to become angry and his voice became harsh. Eventually as we looked at Mark we could see another outline appearing around him. We could see lapels forming on his shoulders, and pockets, it was as if he was wearing a uniform.

Mark was shouting "Get out, get away." But it was David he was yelling at because he was winding the spirit up and spirit was talking through Mark.

We were taking photographs and at one point Mark's head wasn't even there. All we could see was a shadow. We picked a lot of emotion up in that place. All the suffering and it kept coming back to just this one police officer. We occasionally heard chains while we were in there. Some did a form of ouija, using a glass. I did sit down at the table, but didn't touch it. I kept hearing someone saying – "danger, danger, danger."

The building is close to St Editha's church in Tamworth so we also went into the graveyards. A couple had a few experiences in there, seeing mists and shapes, but nothing major.

Cards Galore and More was a shop in Attleborough, Nuneaton. It was on three floors and as soon as I went in I could smell cooking. In the shop downstairs the time on the clock kept changing. We picked up that it was an old man who kept changing the clock because he didn't like it. He was a lovely man and Julie, the owner, had nicknamed him Ron. On the top floor there was a lady crying because a child had died and on the middle floor the smell of cooking was at its strongest. Spirit were all of the same family. She was crying for the baby she had lost, but she was also doing the cooking.

Another interesting place is the Falstaff Museum on Sheep Street in Stratford-upon-Avon. It is an old Tudor building situated on five Ley Lines. There has been a building on this spot since 1146. One such building was called The Shrieve's House, which was named after it's owner, William Shrieve, who was an archer to Henry VIII. It was also the home of the 1st Mayor of Stratford and has been used by the military and army. During Shakespeare's time it was a tavern and brothel, and it is believed that William Shakespeare was a regular visitor there.

Outside is the Witch's Courtyard, where they burned witches hundreds of years ago and that is where I felt most things were. One of my colleagues on Spirits of the Night was physically pushed on the staircase, but I was just happy to sit outside in the courtyard where I could feel I was surrounded by loads of women. I really enjoyed sitting there. I felt at home. One of the other mediums asked me why I kept wanting to go out there and I said that I just felt I could have loads of conversations with all the ladies that were there.

"Well you're in the right place because they're all sitting with you," he said.

And they certainly were. I could feel them all there. At first I could just hearing them chanting. Then they started talking about their lives and how they hadn't meant any harm, but people took it all wrong because they concocted spells and made herbal remedies.

The investigation did prove a long one though. Usually our nights would go from about nine in the evening to anything between two and four in the morning. But with the Falstaff Museum we were coming out when people were going in for their morning coffees.

Sheryl didn't really get anything. She felt it was because the place is set up as a museum. As we walked through the rooms there were bits of material and curtains hanging down, with taped noises, such as things cackling at you, as you walked down the stairs. It's made to look eerie so it spoilt the feeling of the place as far as we were concerned. For instance on one staircase there was a huge grizzly bear which just seemed out of place.

Sometimes we just pick up feelings and atmosphere, not people. Smethwick Baths was such an example. Years ago, from March to October, it was an indoor swimming pool. Then, in the winter months, the pool was covered over to turn it into a dance hall. But, as I have said, we didn't know the history of the place before we went. All we knew was that we could feel music and the joviality there. That it had been a happy place.

The lower floor was vast. There were big columns and we could hear a machine running, which we thought was something to do with when it had been the baths. During WW2 it had been both an air raid shelter and a hospital. The first lot of casualties from the air raids had been brought here to be treated before being moved elsewhere. However we only picked up the presence of airmen. Here, downstairs, it was quite a sad place because of what it had been used for. But upstairs was a really happy place.

We didn't use ouija boards but here we used something similar. A breadboard with a huge spring on it with a smaller piece of board on the top. All we had to do was put a finger on it to see if it would move. That was the first time the board was ever used, but I didn't stay in the room to witness anything. Apparently nothing happened and the board was never mentioned again.

The Salutation Inn in Nottingham is my one regret because I just can't do claustrophobic places. It's a pub now but parts of the building date back to 1240 when it was built on top of numerous underground caves. In the 1500's and 1600's it became a hiding place for anyone trying to escape persecution. There was also a colony of lepers there and then later in the 1700's it was frequented by highwaymen.

When you go in it's as active as hell and you can go down through tunnels which lead right under Nottingham Castle. There are also secret waterways, a waterfall and stalagmites. But I just couldn't do anything. I tried my hardest, but I just couldn't go down there because it was such an enclosed space. So I sat on the stairs talking to myself while everyone else were all down below, filming and such-like. But I got a lot from just sitting on the steps.

The tunnels date back to Robin Hood's time and old smugglers were telling me how they smuggled the tobacco and the drinks, even bodies. They told me how they travelled on boats underneath the castle and would hide everything in the old cellars of the pub. They said how easy it was to smuggle all these goods and that virtually nobody got caught. And I was told how they used to transport people from Nottingham Castle out through the tunnels. All the ghost hunters were down in the cellars below looking for activity and there was I sitting on the steps with them all chatting to me.

Spirit world

Spirit World is a very, very strange thing.

From the age of three I have spoken to spirit. It just always seemed normal to me. I'd see someone or someone would walk into the room and I'd just acknowledge them. Now over the years that I have sat opposite someone in my kitchen, hundreds of spirits have visited me. I really don't know why I've been chosen, I can never answer that question, but it's just lovely that they trust me. Whether it's a child or an adult, a sad spirit or an angry one, they all come to me. And I've had people from all walks of life come to my house for a reading. From celebrities to people looking for answers or wanting fulfilment, even people who have had loved ones murdered. I never know who will be knocking on my door.

As I said I have had celebrities coming to my door. But I'm hopeless and don't recognise them or know who they are. One day I was seeing someone out and knew by his car he was someone special. But I didn't know how famous he was, until I saw Steve's face as he arrived at the front door as this gentleman was leaving. He was speechless and kept saying afterwards – "did you really not know who that was?"

I relate exactly what spirit tells me, whether its good or bad. I believe I've been chosen for a reason and if I hold back on anything I'm not doing my job. I'm sure there are times I could be hung, drawn and quartered because things just come out without me thinking. But I feel, because I'm their tool, if I don't get it correct in their way of saying it, I'm not doing it right. Even to this day anything that is said to me I just pass it on.

I would never split a relationship up but sometimes I'm told to say – "oh you need to get rid of them." Although I always think that perhaps I shouldn't be saying it, I do, and then afterwards people tell me that their life is ten times better. So I just go with spirit and whatever they tell me I just relate it.

People just want to know their loved ones are around them and I feel so much satisfaction when I get a phone call to say, "oh it's wonderful I'm not in this dark place any more." I'm told I've got a big soft heart, which I know I have, but I'll help anybody and anything to do with spirit. If spirit is there then I'll do it, because I'm being used for a reason and I love the feedback I get. My husband takes phone calls where people say "oh tell Carol she was spot on." To me that's great.

Some people come from far afield to see me. I've had a lady from Cardiff come regularly and another from Aberystwyth, who I told years ago would live in Wales and she just laughed at me then. Someone else comes from Exeter to see me. And someone came all the way from New York.

When I give my readings the voices of spirit often sound all the same although I can usually tell the difference between a man and a woman and a child. Of course I also see them, so then I know whether it's a man or a woman, young or old. Although some do just chose to talk to me, but I can tell by their voices if they're younger or older. And sometimes, instead of telling me something is going to happen, they actually show me. Like when someone is going to be signing any papers or such-like.

If there is more than one spirit at a reading they do often talk to each other. And sometimes I have had conflict where a husband and wife have divorced many years previously and maybe I've had their son or daughter in the kitchen. They will both come in but will stay apart from each other, they might even have a row. I have had that happen. One accusing the other of knowing something the other didn't know.

Sometimes I can give what is known as a cross reading. This is where spirit is talking about something or somebody which the person in front of me can't relate to. They then go away and tell a friend and that friend realises they can relate to it. It's spirit's way of trying to get someone to come for a reading.

A lot of mediums will hold something belonging to someone in spirit world. I don't like doing that because it can be very obvious if it belonged to a man or a woman. Particularly a piece of jewellery. It's easy to tell from the size and shape of a ring who it belonged to, and a necklace is even more obvious. I prefer the person sitting opposite to keep hold of an item and not tell me what it is. Spirit will often tell me about it anyhow. Once I was told – "she's got my wedding ring on a chain around her neck."

But early on I did feel I wanted something to use as a prop and someone suggested I use cards. When I was a child my dad used to take me to New Brighton and we always had a go on the 'hook-a-duck'. Once I won a set of playing cards but thought no more of them. Then one day I found them in my house. How they had got there I don't know but I started using them. Then when my mother died I went into her house and into her bedroom. She hadn't got a lot apart from junk jewellery and suchlike but when we came home Steve said to me "I found these," and he produced a set of cards.

"My mum didn't play cards," I said.

"That's what I thought," he said.

My mum must have wanted me to have them, so I started using them as well. Now I give people the choice of which out of the two packs they want to use.

They are really just a prop but I make sure they are used in the right way. First the person must shuffle them and then divide them into three piles. They then take seven cards from wherever they want and place them on the table in front of me. We go through the whole pack in this way until the end of the reading which usually takes about an hour. Spirit world tells me the significance of each card. If they are the future, the past or the present. The cards run alongside side spirit world who are helping the person pick the right card. But each card can mean different things to another person. Someone could pick the Ace of Hearts up and it could be upside down. So I say "you're moving," but the next person could pick the Ace of Hearts up and it could mean they're not moving. The cards go with the individual personality. I know it sounds strange but that's the way it works, the cards don't necessarily mean anything specific its just what spirit makes of them.

But having all these spirits visit me can be problematic. They live off energy. Very often after readings I switch a light on and 'bang!' the light bulb will go.

On just a normal day spirit might be around just listening and that can effect the lights too. I was sitting chatting with a friend of mine the other day, not giving her a reading, just having a chat but it got very dark so I put the big light on. It started humming and flashing and I'm sure it was them listening to me. One of the lights in the kitchen isn't as bright as the others, although I have changed the bulb. And when I turn them off. That one stays on for a short while after the others have gone out. And I'm used to things disappearing then turning up in strange places. If I lose scissors I usually find them in the garden. They love metal you see. It's the electricity. A conductor.

Sometimes they do things which even amaze me. For my daughter Natalie's 30th birthday her best friend wanted me to send some photographs over for her. Now I love photos and memories and we've got a cupboard upstairs where I keep all my albums. We've got loads so when we got them all out they were everywhere, all over the place. We were looking for her birth book, the album covering her 0-5 years, so I could send some off to her friend. But we couldn't find it anywhere.

I thought maybe my elder daughter Gemma had still got it from my 60th birthday the previous year. But no she hadn't. Which meant I had to phone Natalie to ask if she'd got any of the photo albums. No she hadn't, but of course she wondered why I was asking.

A few days later we came home and Steve said I'm going in the loft, it's got to be in there. I went into the conservatory where Steve had vacuumed that morning and there was a book on the floor. I called to him asking why he'd left it on the floor.

"I haven't," he said, coming in, "I put everything away and vacuumed earlier."

He insisted there had been nothing there when he tidied up but when he picked the album up, he went white. It was Natalie's 0-5 book lying there in the middle of the floor.

I've had a lot of things transported but not normally something as big as a photo album. Yet another particular item really surprised me.

The cards I use for my readings are kept in a small gold coloured tin box. Also in that tin is a ring which has never been out of that tin since it turned up there many years ago. My mum died in October 1998 and we went away the following month to Lanzorote. While I'm away I always wrap my box of cards and my ball in black velvet and store them in the loft.

On my first morning back to work I got them down and started to lay them out. I like to give them a chance to energise before my first reading. To my surprise there was a ring in the box. When I took it out and looked at it I recognised it as my mum's eternity ring. A week later my sister telephoned to tell me she'd lost mum's eternity ring. She said she'd lost it in the salon while washing someone's hair. It had gone down the drain.

"So I'm going to have to get a plumber in to see where it is," she said.

"I think I've got it," I told her.

She couldn't believe it.

So that ring was transported from Liverpool to Tamworth and I've never taken it out of that box since because, I feel that's the place it should be. It was like I was meant to have it. With my mum and my dad not believing in what I did, how strange that it appeared in the box I keep my cards. But, like my dad, did my mum believe in the end too? The night she died she was critical and I didn't get to her in time but my nieces were with her. They said that mum was worrying about a little girl at the end of the bed because she thought she was going to fall off. She said the little girl was waving so she waved back. So even she saw something just before she died. Then she asked for a whisky. The nurse brought her some water. She said it was lovely – "the best whisky I've had." Then she just went to sleep and peacefully died.

But one incredible story of transportation involved a gentleman who came to see me for a reading.

When he first came in he said "I'm not quite sure why I'm here but I've been intrigued by what people have said about you. So I thought I'd give it a go."

He lived on a farm which had been his father's and his parents had lived in a bungalow on the drive leading to the farmhouse. He'd lost his mum and dad within three months of each other and he and his sisters hadn't been into that bungalow since but I told him spirit was saying they must go in. Then we suddenly heard the sound of breaking glass. The first thing I thought of was that the bottle of red wine, which I had on the corner of my kitchen shelf, had been knocked over so I jumped up to look. But it was perfectly intact. I looked around to see what could have made the noise and then spotted a small piece of red glass, slightly larger than a sweet.

"Where's that come from?" I said. "Nothing's broken."

"Well I heard it too," the gentleman commented. "And it doesn't mean anything to you?"

"No, nothing. It must be for you." I joked.

"I don't think so," he said.

I thought about it then said – "Well tell you what I'll put it behind the wine and if you ever want it you know where it is."

I finished his reading, which he thoroughly enjoyed, saying it was like therapy and he would definitely come again the left.

A couple of weeks went by then one Monday he phoned me up.

"Do you remember that piece of red glass?" he asked. "Have you still got it?"

I told him I had so he said that he was going to be in my area the next day so could he pick it.

"Yes," I said. "Is there a purpose for it?"

"Purpose? I'll tell you when I come."

So he came and he had one of his sisters with him. She told me she'd been dying to meet me and that I wouldn't believe what had happened.

"When he got home," she told me. "He said we needed to go into the bungalow because Carol says we must."

They opened the door to find there was a leak and water was running everywhere. Luckily everything was saved and they managed to clean it all up. But, on walking in, the first thing they spotted was their mother's big red vase standing on a table in the hallway. And there was a big hole in it. He couldn't believe it because when he took the piece of glass from my house he discovered it matched and fitted exactly.

A lot of people are frightened to die but I have philosophies that I always live by and as I've already said one of those is that we never die alone. So many times during a reading I see someone in a hospital who is looking towards a corner. If you ask what they're looking at they'll say – "So-an-so's there." Or they're completely out-of-it then all of sudden their eyes open and they're looking across the room as if there's someone there. I'm a true believer spirit are around us when we're ill or when something happens or if we're feeling down. We've all been put here for a reason and there's always a story for each individual.

I don't like technology but I do believe it has made it easier for spirit to energise into a photograph. This is my philosophy number two and as I've said I have so many photographs in which I can see spirit. But it doesn't always happen with just me. Someone once sent me a photograph of their nan who had come through in their readings. It was taken on the day she died and there, by the fireplace, is an image of her husband who had come to fetch her.

There was one occasion when I went out into my garden to take some photographs. One photograph, just one photograph, contained a colourful misty mass. It was a cloudy day so it wasn't a reflection from the sun, or the sun's glare, but at the moment I took the photograph there was an accident out in the road at the back of my house involving a bike. We did hear that someone had died. The photo I had taken a minute later was completely clear.

White noise, found in so many modern appliances, is also something which can attract spirit. A gentleman came to me who had actually been coming to me for a few years. During this particular reading I kept being told that "he was listening." This gentleman then told me he had lost his son quite tragically, and very quickly, with cancer at a young age. This young man had only got married the year before he died and his wife had only just given birth to their first child. Naturally the grandparents were helping as much as they could and he told me the only way they could get the baby to sleep was by playing white noise. One night he put the baby down and sat down for a while. Then as he listened he suddenly realised he could hear his son's voice talking to the child, encouraging him to go to sleep – "be good now and go to sleep," the voice kept saying.

I saw a lady named Lisa who said she'd never done anything like this before but as soon as we started her mum came straight through. During the reading something was said about opera and Alexa suddenly came on. All the time I've been working that has never happened before. The voice suddenly said – "this is for your mum. Unfortunately we haven't got Amazon music but we can play this." And it started playing a piece from an opera.

Lisa said, "does that happen a lot?"

"No," I said. "It's never happened before."

So she left and the next lady came in and someone came through, who apparently I used to see, and whenever we hit on something the lady could accept, my cooker would ping.

Spirit has no concept of time, none what-so-ever, and you can often see them during the day as well as at night. But there is one particular time that they do seem to like and that is around 3 o'clock in the morning. This is another philosophy of mine. Without a doubt if you're in a dream, or whatever, between three and a quarter to four in the morning that is the time they come to you. We can be woken for no reason and wonder why but it is in that short period of time that our subconscious mind is linked to them. The next quarter of an hour is when our mind goes back.

I don't like doing readings over the telephone. It just doesn't feel right for me. I just can't feel the vibes. I have to be with that person. But I did have a phone call during the Covid pandemic from a lady who said she'd been to see me loads of times. As the conversation started I was very conscious of spirit being with me.

"I do feel I do need to speak to you," I said. "Somebody died yesterday at 6.30."

It was her mum. I gave her the best reading I could, she loved it and thought it was brilliant, but it just wasn't right for me.

There is one other reading I did over the telephone and although it was some time ago, it sticks in my mind because it was one reading I was really proud of. A lady phoned me from Toronto saying that I did all her family's cards so could I do a telephone reading? I'd never done a telephone reading before but I said I'd give it a go. To help with the reading I was sent a photograph. It was a beautiful photograph of a group of Asian ladies. They all looked so lovely in their saris but I was drawn to one lady in particular. She was in the middle and was wearing a green sari.

On the appointed day and time I received the phone call and holding the photograph I commented that I was drawn to this lady in particular.

The person on the other end of the telephone said "why with all the ladies in the photograph have you gone for her?"

I said I didn't know I just felt really drawn to her and I was getting something connected to Marks and Spencers and in particular, Marks and Spencers black trousers. I also felt that her jewellery was missing and that she'd been hurt on her arms.

Then it came to me – "she's no longer with us is she?"

No was the answer.

"She's been murdered hasn't she?" I said and could then hear people in the background crying.

I was asked if I could pick anything up. First of all I could see a lime-ash floor, then double-doors that were white, but behind the doors I knew the police had missed evidence.

"Was she hurtled into a car," I asked.

"Yes," was the answer, "wearing Marks and Spencers black trousers."

I was also told that her bangles had been tugged from her arms causing her arms to bleed. So that's why they were sore.

"But they've got the wrong person," I said.

"This is why I wanted this reading," she said. "But can I phone you back in a week."

That following week I received her second call. The person originally charged had been released and her husband had been arrested. After my phone call forensics had been sent back in. They searched the lime-ash floor and behind the white double doors and on the double doors they discovered they'd missed some DNA.

I also prefer to give one to one readings. The trouble with public readings in a theatre or such-like, the medium has to go quickly from one member of the audience to another because that is what the crowd expects. I couldn't do that. I would have to stay with the person I'm talking to. I did attend a theatre event once and was introduced to the medium giving the event.

"Oh hello," I said. "You've just booked a holiday?"

Taken aback he jokingly said "Do you want to take the show tonight?"

"But you're not sure about it," I continued, referring to the holiday.

"Two-and-a-half hours ago I booked to go to Crete," he said. "And now my partner's fallen out with me."

I work in my kitchen because there seems to be so much energy in it. I think it's because we're situated on the leylines of two churches. One in Stonydelph, the other in Holy Trinity, Wilncote. And we're smack in the middle. So that is probably where the kitchen gets all the energy from.

I have met lovely people during the course of my work, but not all come willingly. There was a young man who I'd never seen before. As he sat down in front of me he said "I don't even know why I'm here. My mother booked this."

But I started going deep into his life and he was in tears. He told me he'd been to see therapists but didn't feel they had helped at all "but I come to you," he said, "and I'm pouring my heart out and crying my eyes out. You brought my granddad through, you know everything about him and what I've got at home that's his. That means the world to me."

One particular older gentleman came straight to the point – "I'm here because I've been given your number. I don't believe in all this rubbish so no disrespect to you but I'm sitting here for ten minutes and if you don't give me anything I'm going through that door."

So we started and very soon I could see someone touching his leg. He felt it himself because he said "my left leg's gone funny." I told him that I was glad he had said that because I was going to ask him about the lady........ As soon as I said "lady," he was taken aback and said "what do you mean a lady?"

It turned out that his wife had been taken into hospital. It was at the time of the pandemic and she was put on a covid ward so he wasn't allowed to visit. He then received a call to say she was going to die. They didn't know how long she'd got but they would phone him when it was time so he could spend her last minutes with her.

Sadly he didn't get those last minutes because she went too quickly in the end and the staff were so busy. But he was allowed to see her and I could tell him things about that visit and about the room she was in. He couldn't believe how I knew and kept saying – "How would you know that."

Then she gave me her name, not just her first name, but her whole name. She talked about the new kitchen he'd had. I said "she loves the kitchen but she doesn't like the colour." And he told me that when he picked it out he'd said "she's not going to like the colour."

As he left he said "You're my life-line now. Can I come back."

It always makes me happy when someone says that.

A girl came once who took me completely by surprise as she was quite abrupt.

"I don't really need to be here," she said as she stepped through the door.

I couldn't help myself and curtly replied – "Then why are you here?"

"Well I thought I'd just give it a go but I've got no problems in my life, none whatsoever."

I led her through to the kitchen and started the reading. Almost immediately I spotted a lady behind her. When I mentioned it she was turning around and saying she couldn't see anything.

"You're having me on. There's no one there," she kept saying

But I could see a young lady with long dark hair who I was told had died from cancer. When I told my visitor this she immediately knew who it was and kept saying "I don't believe this, I don't believe it."

It was her best friend and she asked if she was alright.

"Yes she's fine," I said "absolutely fine."

I told her that her friend had been to a cafe someone had just bought and it was the best cup of coffee she'd had. It turned out her mother and brother had just bought a cafe in Tamworth. So after coming and saying I don't know why I'm here, when she was leaving, she was saying – "when can I come again?"

A man came and said "I've been here before. And when I came in your first words to me were – 'Oh dear. You've booked a very expensive cruise. But you're not going on it.'"

He said he remembered saying to me that he had booked and paid for it so he would be going on it.

I'd said "Well you're not going on it. I don't know why, but that cruise on the 24th of March will be cancelled."

A few weeks later the country was hit by Covid and on the 22nd of March we went into lock-down and everything was cancelled. He also said I'd told him he would retire at 50. Which he has now decided he'll do as he's a company director and he's selling his business.

A lady came to see me saying – "you're my last hope."

As we started spirit told me she was going through a complete mental breakdown.

"Are you having problems mentally?" I asked.

"Yes," she said.

Spirit then told me she'd got a bag full of Valium. I couldn't believe it but when I mentioned it she opened her bag and showed me. She told me she'd come to me because she felt, in a previous life, she'd killed numerous children. That she was a bad person so needed to kill herself to get out of this life to find the bad person she had been. I said to her "you're not a bad person at all," and with that her mother came through. She gave her daughter a lecture that she wasn't this demon witch or wicked person who had killed all these children at all.

If I can help someone, or spirit can, I will so I told her I was only a phone call away. Every week when she got these bad thoughts she would phone me and I would talk her through it.

I also told her she needed to move house, because it was the house which was suffocating her.

"And when you move house," I said. "You will marry your partner."

So she bought a bungalow on the other side of town and got married. Like so many other readings this ended happily for the person concerned which gives me so much pleasure.

Sometimes a reading can have me in tears. I had a young man in his 20's come to see me who had been once before when he was 18. It was because of what had happened to him that had brought him back. The minute he walked in I was getting all this 'babble-babble-babble' in my ears.

I looked at him and said "you've just had some deaths. Not just one death, but more than one"

He looked at me and nodded his head. Straight away there was a gentleman in the room and I was getting that this gentleman had died first. It was his dad who had gone into hospital for just a routine operation. Before going in he had actually said "I'm going to catch Covid while I'm in hospital." His son had said there was no reason why he should. But he did, and he died.

Then I said to the young man – "He's got hold of a lady's hand."

He then told me he'd just lost his mum too. She had said to him "I don't feel very well," and as he didn't think she looked very well called an ambulance. In the ambulance he sat holding her hand and as they were travelling to the hospital she opened her eyes and said "your Dad's here." Then she smiled, looked at him and just went.

But things got worse. Although there was only the lady and gentleman in the room I sensed that somewhere there was a small child in spirit world who had drowned. He then told me about his little girl who was aged about 3. Her mother had opened the door to let her go out and play in the garden. They had got a very shallow water feature. It had only got 2 inches of water in it but she had tripped and fallen face down in it and drowned. I was really crying in the kitchen with him. He asked me if she was ok but all I could tell him was that she was safe.

I kept getting the letter M. That was his mother whose name was Margaret. She was the reason he had come back and the fact that his dad had been in the ambulance with them. He said he'd had a really good reading when he was younger. That I'd told him all about his career and what he would be doing but he admitted that when he first came to see me – "I was a naughty boy" so thought he would never do all that. But he had. He'd graduated, done this, done that, and had got a beautiful wife.

Ironically he was the only reading I did that morning, the others hadn't turned up for some reason. So it seems that all my energies were sent to focus on him. I was crying with him in the kitchen.

I don't remember many of my readings but that one will stick in my head forever.

Once again I felt I was given the proof, via someone else, of my philosophy that we never die alone. Another comes to mind.

We had some neighbours who we were very friendly with and one day I looked at him and said, "You don't look very well, do you think you should go to the doctor."

"Oh I'm all right Carol," he said.

A few days later an ambulance appeared outside their house. His wife kept saying it was his stomach but I just felt there was something wrong with his lungs. When we visited him in hospital I suggested he should have a lung X Ray. I really felt the problem was there. It turned out they were doing one the next day. Then the next day we got the news that he'd got lung cancer. He ended up in a hospice and one day asked to see me and Steve. He was very weak and it reminded me of when I was with my dad.

He said my name so I took his hand and he said "I've seen my mum."

"Well," I said, "when she comes you go with her."

He smiled and said "Thank you. I'm not afraid any more."

He had never believed in anything I did but, again, in that last minute he did.

One of Gemma's friends, Clare, said a gentleman called Tom wanted to come and see me. He owned one of the pubs in Tamworth and had been to see loads of mediums but wasn't happy with any of them. So he decided to come and see me although he felt I wouldn't be any different to any of the others. Especially 'if I just worked in a kitchen.'

So he arrived and I immediately said to him that the pub had got spirits in it.

"Yes," he said sarcastically, "loads of them. In bottles."

"No," I said. "There's a man called Richard. Actually there's a Richard and a William."

Needless to say he was pleased with his reading in the end and all the family members I had picked up.

A few days later Steve and I wanted to go somewhere to eat after a day out, so decided to go to his pub. We got ourselves a drink and sat down. As I looked around I could see a figure standing by the bar. It was a man.

Steve looked at me and said, "you can see something can't you."

"Yes I said. He's trying to hide behind a cupboard."

Tom came over and said he could see I was fidgeting. "Is everything all right?"

So I told him I could see someone.

"Who is it?" he asked.

"I think it's this Richard."

Some days later I went back and Tom's partner, Harvey, was there so he came over to speak to me.

"You're the medium aren't you?"

"Yes."

"Can you describe Richard?" he asked.

"Well he's not an old man, William is the oldest and he's something to do with the castle."

I told him that felt I wanted to stand over by the hatch at the bar. So he took me over.

"There's a door there." I said.

"No it's just a wall."

"No there is definitely a door there."

"That's interesting," he said. "Let's go through to the other room."

I had actually been in the cellar of this pub before when I worked with one of the groups so I knew everywhere was red. The same colour as inside the castle. And that there are tunnels leading to the castle from the pub. And I told him.

"Oh that's interesting," he said. "So what would this room have been used for."

"Smuggling," I said.

Then I pointed to a shape in the wall. "Look at that."

"Oh yes. There must have been a door there."

Richard, I think, was a twin and he died a couple of years previous to my visit from cancer. And he had died in the pub as he used to work there and was always down that end.

Gemma said they'd told his brother and he couldn't believe it.

I had two friends who came to see me regularly called June and Veronica. They'd been coming to see me for years travelling from Machynlleth in Wales. They would leave at 3 o'clock in the morning. Stop at the services for breakfast. Then come to me. On a visit in December 2022 Veronica told me she had lost her sister since she had last seen me. Her sister lived in Shropshire and unbeknown to her, somehow, friends had persuaded her to change her will and leave everything to the church. I remembered seeing Veronica previously and giving her some names. One was a Scottish name and that turned out to be the solicitor involved in the will.

After the cremation Veronica had taken her sister's ashes back home with her and put them on the window sill. She asked me what I thought she should do with them.

"I don't know," I said. "Let her decide. She'll tell me or she'll find a way of letting you know."

So during the course of Veronica's reading her sister said – "When you go sweetie they can put the ashes together and we'll go off a big cliff."

"How weird," she said. "I had a dream recently where I fell off a cliff."

Later as we chatted she told me she was going to Liverpool. I asked her who she was going with and she told me her daughter. I then got a message to tell her to be careful of a fall.

"You're going to have a fall," I said. "But I feel we can stop this happening."

"Well if you're going to fall, you're going to fall, aren't you Carol," she replied.

"Yes but they're telling me we can stop this happening."

She just laughed it off but I said that her daughter would say to her – "Are you all right?" and she would say three times – "I think so, but I'm not sure."

Four or five weeks later I get a phone call from June to say that Veronica had died. She had a fall on the Albert Dock in Liverpool. Her daughter went to pick her up saying "Are you all right?" and Veronica said "I'm all right. I think so. I think so. I think so."

June also said that the following week her family were taking both ashes to a cliff down south somewhere and were going to throw them off.

Visits now from June can be quite emotional because Veronica always joins us in the room.

People's ashes are often mentioned in readings. One lady had her friend come through and I asked if anything had been done about her friend's ashes.

"Not yet, no." She said.

"Well she wants to go to Caernarvon where the boats are."

"Nobody knows that." Was the answer. "How did you know."

Sometimes a reading can take me by complete surprise. When a gentleman by the name of Marcus came to see me I immediately heard a voice say "hello Carol," and I thought – I know that voice.

"Darling, it's me," she said in the most beautiful, softest voice.

I just knew I knew the voice and I was obviously thinking out loud because Marcus said "What did you just say?"

But the lady continued – "tell him I just love those drawings. They're absolutely spectacular."

He looked at me then explained that it was his mother Mary, a lovely lady who used to come to me for readings. I remembered her then and also remembered one particular reading I gave her.

When she had last come to see me she was desperate to die in order to be with her loved one. I told her to make the most of the next few months and to make sure "you do this for the right children and not the wrong one." It turned out that she had one son who just didn't care about her, he hadn't even gone to her funeral, so before she died she had changed her will.

"I'm with my good man now, we're back together" she said. "I feel fabulous, I'm with him, and we're together. And we've been put together."

Apparently she had kept her husband's ashes so after she had been cremated her children had mixed both sets of ashes together, which had really pleased her.

Although there was one thing that hadn't pleased her, but she did see the funny side of it.

"I don't like sunflowers darling," she said. "But they put a sunflower in with me. And they did it deliberately."

She told me how I had kept her lifeline open with her late husband and now I had to keep that lifeline open with her children. Which will happen because Marcus said – "Me and my sister will come to you for the remainder of your life."

This was one of the loveliest readings I did but it was also very emotional. I usually can cope with anyone who sits in with me getting upset, but it's spirit world I can't cope with because you can't be seen to be putting your arm around them. When she spoke to me I could feel her and even Marcus could feel something because he said "the whole room's gone red-hot."

She had come through to me very quickly because she had only been cremated the week before. But this is not that unusual. I've had a few readings when people have only just passed. And it always seems to be on a Friday. Very often one of my Friday readings will find someone whose funeral hasn't even taken place.

I love my job. I love meeting people. And I feel if I can help people, to me that's the most important thing. A lady came to see me one August who had just got over a terrific divorce. She phoned me six months later to remind me that at the time I was adamant she would meet somebody. This was one time that I had doubted myself. We were in between the lockdowns of 2020 but spirit insisted she would meet someone. I even described him, and said that she would meet him somewhere strange. Then I told her she would get married in February.

At the beginning of the following February she telephoned to say she'd met somebody in September, in a petrol station of all places, had spent the whole of October with him, and she was now getting married the following week. She said she'd never been so happy in her life.

This is one of many incidents. I've predicted babies and there have been times when doctors have said ladies couldn't have babies and the next thing there's a little baby born. I've told women what the sex of their baby was, sometimes when they've been told something different by the doctors. I once said that someone was having a girl.

"But I've been told it's a boy," she said.

The next thing she'd had a scan and the doctors told her they had got it wrong and that she was actually having a little girl, not a little boy.

I once gave a reading to someone who has actually now become a friend. The first time I met her I told her she would become pregnant.

'No, no, no,' she said as they'd told her fertility treatment may be needed.

But every time she came to see me I told her she was going to get pregnant and that she would have four children. She has now got four children and all by natural means.

Another lady was told she couldn't have children but I stopped her taking some medication. Thank goodness she did because she was pregnant and if she had continued taking the tablets she would have had a miscarriage. After that her husband sent me a huge bouquet of flowers. I also said it would be a little boy and his name would be associated with strength. They named him Alexander.

I told another man that he would fall out with his mother but that he would meet someone and would have children with this lady, two beautiful boys. Which he did. He always says to me that – "even though you've got to know me, when I come, you always know the next part of my life that's going to happen." One week he phoned me to say that he and his wife had split up, and he was going through a really bad divorce, but that he'd got his mum back. Which is exactly what I had told him during his previous reading.

I've predicted all sorts of things. Even that houses will be built at various places, which they have. And although I didn't realise it at the time, spirit was warning me about Covid.

In 2019 I was told someone I knew would be ill and was shown the letter 'C'. Of course at the time I naturally assumed it was cancer. However it wasn't cancer. It was Covid. And it turned out to be a good friend of mine called Alan. He was one of the first to be infected by Covid and was on a life support machine for a long time. Although suffering from long Covid he is all right now. I was also told I would be very poorly and on the 16th of October 2020 I also contracted Covid.

I was told there would be problems for Steve in relation to his work and low and behold on the 26th of January 2020 he went to work to be told they were closing the place down. He had worked there for 44 years. It did take twelve months, but it was twelve months of Steve not knowing whether he was coming-or-going.

I'm also a believer that spirit will show themselves in different forms, like animals or birds, even butterflies. You see a robin, and that could be your mum. I know my mum comes to me in the form of a robin. But sometimes those animals can be quite a surprise.

I did a reading one winter. Caterpillars don't exist in the winter but I found myself saying "watch for the caterpillar." The person who I was giving the reading to agreed with me. Caterpillars only appear in the summer. But I still kept seeing this caterpillar crawling along the side of a path. A few days later I got a phone call. He'd found a caterpillar crawling along a path in his garden and they actually put it in a jam jar. That would certainly be a symbol from spirit world.

I've had many people in my kitchen who say 'no, no I can't take that'. But spirit will continue and continue repeating themselves in order to get their point across. They really nag me, saying "you tell them, you tell them. They've got to do this, they've got to sort that out etc."

One spirit became very insistent about a photograph. But the lady couldn't understand what her dad was trying to tell her. He persevered and kept telling me about a photograph that had been moved from one room to, as he put it, 'the room which she used as an office.' It wasn't in a frame, but was propped up against another which was in a frame. She kept saying she couldn't think of a photograph of her father under these circumstances. When she got home she realised he was talking about a photograph which had been received of a new baby in the family. It had been put on one side when first taken out of the envelope. Then eventually moved to the dining room, the room she used as her office, and propped up against another photograph. And the significance of this, was that her father's name was Francis and the little girl, had been named Frances.

Sometimes people are in my house for reasons other than having a reading, but I still make contact with someone from their life who is in spirit world. I was having some work done one summer and said to the workmen – "Sorry lads but you wont get any more cups of tea because someone's just told me the kettle is going to blow up." Two minutes later one of the workmen had a phone call from his wife to say that their kettle had just blown up.

On that same day I turned around and saw a man in my kitchen so I started talking to him. The one lad asked what was going on so I described the man I was talking to. He was tall, thin and had a little moustache.

"He's wearing heavy-rimmed glasses but he doesn't always wear them." I said.

The lad looked at me and asked if I knew his name.

"Oh now you've asked me he won't tell me." I joked. "But there is the letter L over his head."

"That's my granddad," the lad said. "His name was Leonard."

When I was having my new kitchen installed one of the men working on the kitchen, David, had lost his mum the week he was due to start. I told him he could postpone but he said that, emotionally, he needed to carry on working. On the first day a lady appeared to me at the bottom of the stairs and later at the top of the stairs. From what she said I realised it was his mum. He later showed me a photograph of her and I recognised her immediately. I find it hard to trust people who come to do work for me having been ripped off on many occasions, but she told me he was a good man. From then on I felt comfortable and at ease with him. The kitchen was transformed with no really bad reactions from spirit world. Just completely the opposite. People who came to me afterwards said they felt warm, although some said they felt tingling sensations on parts of their body. Some could hear noises, while others saw flashes of light from the corners of their eyes. There certainly was a different ambiance when I started back to work in my new kitchen.

During the course of that first week Dave became intrigued in what I did and I was able to tell him that his mum was looking after him. She told me her name and also his dad's name which convinced Dave it was his mum. She also told me that he needed to believe in himself more.

"He's a good family man," she said. "There's not a lot like him left around."

She talked about his dogs – he had three dogs and she talked about the beautiful lilies. She said there would be no moves, but that she was worried about someone. That there was going to be changes for his dad. Dave then told me that his dad had handed his notice in at work. He worked in Birmingham but lived in Devon, and travelled. She wanted a message passed on to him, telling him not to worry about his son – "he's a champ," she said. I kept getting something about the clothes in his mum's wardrobe and asked if there was a dressing gown in that wardrobe.

"Yes," he said. "The one she was wearing when she died in hospital."

His wife's name was Kat and I got that someone called Julie was connected to his wife. He was so surprised because his wife knew someone called Julie but had never met her, but she was about to meet her for the first time.

Later he sent me a video which his sister had taken of his niece in their mother's house. As the little girl played on the bed, jumping up and down, there were numerous orbs of light flashing around her. While watching it I looked at the wall of the room and a face appeared. From his description I could tell it was his mum and she was laughing.

But I don't have to be in my kitchen for spirit to visit me. They come at any time, and any place, if there's someone with me they want to talk to.

We went on holiday regularly to Tenerife and stayed in the same hotel for ten years running. On one occasion we were sitting having a drink in the bar. It was very busy and crowded so another couple came and asked if they could join us on the two chairs which were vacant at our table. We got chatting then Steve looked at me and said "Oh my God! No." He knew by the look on my face I was picking up on something. As the evening went on I had to ask this lady if she had just lost someone.

"Yes," she said. "How did you know that?"

So I told her what I did and how I pick up on things.

It was her brother who had died so I could tell her that he was at her side and that he had said "please tell her I'm so sorry I just did not want to carry on."

She looked at me and started crying. He gave me his name and she was crying even more. I apologised and said that I would go.

"No, no, no," she said. "It was only a couple of weeks ago. He hung himself."

She had no explanation of why he did it and had really felt she shouldn't go on holiday, but she had. I described him to her and she said "It is him. Is he ok?"

I replied that he was out of all pain and that he just couldn't have carried on. Her husband thanked me and I made two new friends. The next day she came to thank me and told me she did Reiki healing and wanted to give me a head massage for helping her feel better. We kept in touch for quite some time but then, as often happens, it gradually dwindled off.

Another time I was on a coach tour and I could see a man sitting next to a lady at the side of us and holding her hand. I looked at him and he said "could you tell her I'm ok please." When we got off I went up to her. I needed to because if I'm asked, I have to pass the message on. Otherwise I'm not doing my duty to them.

"Excuse me could I have a word with you." I asked. "Please don't think I'm a lunatic or anything like that but have you just lost your husband?"

She looked at me and said "I don't know you from Adam but yes I have."

"Just to let you know he's at peace. He's fine." I said and left it at that.

It was during the Covid pandemic that I noticed how strange spirit can behave. Perhaps it was because I wasn't working that made them restless. All my electricity went in the conservatory and the alarm stopped working, but the electrician couldn't find a thing wrong with it. At one point I had no backdoor. We'd lock it, but it kept coming open of its own accord. I had a locksmith come and he took all the locking system off the door, then boarded it up. I kept saying to him is this normal for a door to keep opening on its own. He said he'd only ever come across it once before. One night Steve and I were both woken up by a little girl crying. Both of us woke at the same time and both heard exactly the same thing. The pandemic certainly affected them too.

The feedback I get is the most rewarding part of my job, if you can call it a job, It's just such a wonderful feeling giving help and assurance to people. Sometimes it's not even the person who came to see me that rings up. I once I had a telephone call from the friend of someone who had come all the way from Lincolnshire to see me. He had recently lost his wife and his friend said that she didn't know what I'd done to him, but he was a totally different person within twenty-four hours of seeing me.

"It's like you've given him his life back," she said.

I can never see this myself but it's lovely to hear and I think 'oh did I?' But when you actually sit with people and they say – "Carol you're like a therapy I'd rather come here than to a therapist session." That really gets to me, knowing that I'm doing something right.

Recently I had a card pushed through the door with a gift voucher. It read -

"To Carol. Thank you for the last nine years I have come to see you. You have helped me through the darkest of times and I honestly don't think I'd be here still if it wasn't for you. I am so grateful to you and you are very special to a lot of people. From your 9.30 am, Jenny."

Spirits and their loved ones

The people who come to me for readings all have their own stories to tell about what their feelings are and how I help them. When I was writing this book some of those people wanted to put their own thoughts down. I was certainly happy to let them speak for themselves and to tell their own stories. I never ask people's surnames, I just ask them their first name. So first we have a lady called Margaret.

"Tears filled my eyes and gently spilled over down onto my cheeks as I sat in the kitchen and listened to my son talking about his sister's recent wedding, on a particular day in June. He told me how he had walked beside her down the aisle, in a beautiful setting within the Shropshire countryside, and how well behaved his young son had been throughout the day. He commented on how her new husband was 'alright' and made her happy. He commented on the fact that we were 'all going to do it again' the following year.

"Covid restrictions had meant the wedding had been cancelled twice previously, eventually taking place with a reduced number of guests. However, an alternative date had been set for the following year which was to be held to re-enact the wedding with the full guest list.

"He talked in detail about a forthcoming holiday that my husband and I were planning, and our intention to change one of our cars. He described how hard his sister worked at her job, referring to her by name.

He spoke tenderly of his former wife's new found relationship; that he was comfortable with it, and was happy for her. He spoke about my health and that of his father's ongoing diagnosed health condition, stressing the importance for him to continue to take his medication. He continued to speak of his previous scepticism of life after death and spiritualism, referring to it as 'all that rubbish.'

"A very varied, in-depth and thought-provoking range of subjects in one conversation, but a conversation not dissimilar to many held between a mother and a son, you might think.

"However, this was far from an ordinary conversation! I was not sitting at home in my kitchen – nor that of my son. I was sitting in Carol's kitchen – and my son had died two years previously!

"I had visited Carol on several previous occasions, and whilst I had initially been open-minded of her work, having married into a Spiritualist family, I had been made aware of the possibility that there was an afterlife, and there were avenues open for loved ones who had passed over to make communication with those still living.

"I was also conscious of reports of many bogus mediums, or charlatans, who preyed on the vulnerable, always ready to take their money in return for a few words of comfort, hope or reassurance.

"Carol was different! On previous visits, I had always been very careful not to give any information away that could be used in the 'reading'. However, Carol was always able to provide me with information that would have been impossible to know, make up or embellish upon.

"In the previous few years, my life had taken several twists and turns, many of which were unique and totally unexpected. On each of my previous visits, Carol had acted as a conduit for loved ones who had passed away – including my mother, father and a much-loved aunt – and they had provided me with much needed reassurance that particular issues currently in my life at that time, would resolve themselves in a particular way, and in some cases, detailed a course of action that I should take to get me through a particularly tricky situation. And they had been right!

"I had often discussed my experiences with close family members, and whilst my husband and daughter came to have a belief in the after-life, my son had remained mildly interested but extremely sceptical, almost to the point of mocking my belief.

"It was therefore reassuring to hear him say on that particular occasion, in Carol's kitchen, that he was 'fine' – a favoured word he would use to describe any positive situation – and that he now understood my belief in the afterlife.

"On a previous visit, shortly after his death, my son, via Carol, had described his very unusual diagnosis and the circumstance of his passing. He had even referred to the very unusual nickname he was called, only known to and used by his closest friends.

"It can be very upsetting for passed loved ones to make contact, but it can also be reassuring for the living to know they are still around, although unseen.

"At the time of my son's untimely, premature and unpredictable death, he left a six week old baby boy, who is growing up to look like his dad, and has certainly inherited his dad's sense of humour! Certain mannerisms and characteristics have manifested themselves in the youngster, which, because of his very young age at the time of his father's death, could not have developed through mimicry. Through my grandson, my son will live on for another generation.

"My life will never be the same, nor as I had planned or envisaged, but it is a great comfort to know that my son is still around and watching over us as a family. Whilst I know that I will never again be able to have physical conversations with my son, I know that he will be able to tell me exactly what he thinks, and show me the way forward through whatever obstacles life puts in my path – providing, of course, Carol is still available to act as that conduit or 'medium' for conversation."

Now there is Vanessa who has also been coming to me for some years now.

"One July night in 2017 I sat watching as my mum slowly passed away. 'She can still hear you,' her carers kept telling me, 'so talk to her.' So I did. Telling her what I had been doing that weekend just like any normal visit but I also kept reminding her that I would be seeing Carol in September.

"Mum never wanted to visit Carol herself, but she always wanted to know all about my visit as soon as I got home from a reading – also trying to explain certain bits of information that Carol had given me or names which had been mentioned. My dad always came through while I was in Carol's kitchen and after one visit Mum smiled when I said he had mentioned the apple pies she always made. He would talk of her a lot and how they missed each other. So, as I sat in her room watching, I prayed that Dad was there with us. Then suddenly, having remained still for so long, and just before she passed away, she lifted her hand. I knew in that instance Dad was there and she was reaching out to him.

"So come September I sat in Carol's kitchen and waited. Carol said how cold she had gone which meant the lady with her had passed within the last six months. I knew then that mum was there. Through Carol she told me that not being able to do things for herself, she had just given up. Something I had felt long before she died. She knew I was there at the end and that my son and his wife had been there earlier. Then she confirmed that Dad was there to fetch her and that she had made a gesture at the time. She said she had missed him every day but had never moaned about it, just talked to him while she was alone.

"I know Dad was there with her by what Carol said, but he stayed quiet on this occasion and let Mum do the talking. Just like it was when they were both alive. Dad just sitting there, nodding in agreement, so I didn't feel disappointed that Dad didn't talk to me like before. On those previous visits to Carol he had always known everything that was going on in the family. Things that Carol just wouldn't have been able to guess at. When my son was getting engaged my mum gave him her engagement ring to give to his girlfriend. Through Carol Dad told me how thrilled he was about that. But Carol was confused as she picked up that my son hadn't actually proposed by the time. "So how has the ring already been chosen?" she asked.

"Later, after the wedding, Mum wondered whether she should give Liz, my daughter-in-law, her eternity ring too but deep down I really wanted to have it. The next time I visited Carol this ring was mentioned and

Carol said it was very important to Dad and that I had to keep it.

"Mum and dad were always both there after Mum's death but, as before and as in life, it was my mum who always did the talking.

"There have been ups-and-downs in my life. Things that Carol could not have known unless someone close to me had told her. She can even mention names in relation to what has been happening to me so I know, while sitting in Carol's kitchen, the people who really knew me, who I may not be able to see any more, are there with me, advising me and talking to me through Carol.

"My Mum loved seeing the first snowdrops appearing in our garden. One of my readings was in a January and Carol mentioned a clump of snowdrops by a stone pot. A few days later I looked out of the kitchen window and there by a stone pot was a clump of snowdrops. I could almost hear my mum saying – "Oh look! The first snowdrops."

Some people do feel nervous when they first come to visit as Liz writes.

"My first visit to Carol I will totally admit, I was terrified. I didn't know what to expect. In fact I was debating whether to go or not. Carol sensed this straight away and was instantly welcoming, reassuring and kind. She explained what she did in great detail and that if I wasn't happy, or didn't enjoy the session, I could leave at any time. But it was very weird because as soon as she began my reading I immediately stopped shaking with nerves and felt relaxed wanting to hear more. Hearing from relatives, like grandparents who had passed away when I was a little girl was so heart-warming. She gave me exact names, places we had been to, jobs we had been doing, and my future partner and son who would be my family a few years later on. Carol was correct in everything. It gave me goosebumps all over. Walking out of her house after that first reading I had a bounce in my step and the biggest smile on my face.

"I have been going to Carol for over ten years now and it brings me comfort to hear from both relatives and pets we have lost over the years. To know they are still ok and looking out for us in their own ways helps me progress for the future.

"Even with my son's autism, family who have passed have guided and supported me throughout Carol's sessions which has taken a weight off my shoulders as it is all new to us. It is good to hear my son is all right and that we're doing everything we should for him as I question myself daily if I'm doing enough.

"I want to thank Carol so much for all the readings for us and the many others she has helped. You are amazing. I believe your readings have helped me a great deal and still help me now. I would recommend her to anyone as she changes lives for the better."

Katie says that "Carol's been in my life since 2005. She has kept me sane after loosing my sister and mum very close together. She is a genuinely honest person. When I have a reading I always feel like a weight has been lifted. She's my therapy. At my first reading Carol got the name I used to call my mum – Betty Boo. She even took a magnet off her fridge before she said the name. She has also related my sister's name, and even her cat's name. She has picked up on dates and anniversaries, family things, future holidays and babies.

At my previous reading to writing this she named my husband's uncle and his father and said that uncle 'has gently asked to let him (my husband) know that he's with his dad and everything is ok.' But what was really incredible was that she once told me to take a photograph at a certain time. She said to say 'cheers' to my husband's uncle. The photograph shows a ball of light on the edge of the photograph."

Another Margaret, admits to having visited other mediums but always comes back to me.

"I have visited Carol for readings on an annual basis now for more than 20 years. She is so friendly and puts you at ease as soon as you step into her home, which is always warm and friendly. She always knows various family members, whether they are in spirit world or not, and we have had some strange names in my family. People say 'it's because you go to see her a lot and she remembers you.' But that's not possible. I go once a year, sometimes it's fifteen months, so she can't possibly remember me from all the other people who visit. Also she only takes your first name.

"I get really excited once I have booked an appointment to see Carol and it can't come quick enough. When I visit Carol I feel close to my family members in the spirit world, like they are in the room next door. Sometimes I have tears, but they are happy tears, and I always feel content when I leave.

"My family have all visited Carol at some time or another and are always on the phone to ask me 'what did Carol say' when I get home.

"During one reading she told me I was going to have an operation, which I did know about. Through Carol my mum told me that they were going to take something out but would also be putting something in. I was confused by this. I had been diagnosed with cervical myelopathy but it got changed to transverse myelitis and this wasn't the operation route. I had to have steroid treatment so I thought that was the something in although nothing coming out. I thought Carol had got it wrong but couldn't believe that.

"The steroid treatment didn't work so within 5 days I was referred back to neurosurgeons to have an operation. It was spinal surgery through the front of my neck to remove two discs and replace with spacers. Something out and something in exactly as Carol had said. I was flabbergasted – she was right again.

"She always brings my ex-husband through and she told me exactly how he passed away and always gives his name. I have a son and daughter. She names them both and their children at different readings. My brother died in Walgrave Hospital awaiting open heart surgery. She told me all about this and also gave me his name. I've had him standing at my side whilst sitting in her kitchen. She's told me he's there. Describing him and once again giving his name.

"I moved into a new house and she described where my kitchen was and things that were in my garden, like the concrete bench at the bottom. She has also told me about holidays. One time she said I would go to Canada. I thought I can't afford to have a holiday like that, but I do have a friend in Canada. As it happened my sister-in-law passed away and left me a small sum of money. My friend in Canada has three sisters here and they invited me to go with them, out of the blue. Carol was right again.

And finally Marcus who has been coming to me for over twenty years. I have already talked about Marcus and his mother Mary but when I told him I was writing a book he was eager to participate -

"We lost my dad in 2003. He was very spiritual and my mum, very religious, but she had the capability of easily following both sides. When my dad Maurice passed away we were all there with him – my mum, my sister, my brother and myself. He had spent the previous week in hospital and we had been there with him talking about all sorts of things. Then just as he was slipping away he said, 'Find a portal that I can get back to you, because I will." So we did and that was Carol.

"We all went once a year, going individually every four months, until 2020, so Carol never realised we were related. Over that time, as a family, we have probably made fifty visits and every time Carol gives us the exact date dad died. Now my dad knew there were alot of charlatans out there so he said that he would always tell us things that nobody else would know. So something personal would come out to each one of us during these visits. She would come up with names of various people that Dad, and us, had had contact with, when we changed cars, the colour of the car, when people were going on holiday, all sorts of things. Nothing life-changing but, what it did give us, was comfort and help with our individual grieving. You see I don't think we ever grieved properly over dad. Mum thought she'd got to be strong for us and we thought we'd got to be strong for her.

"Then for some reason my brother turned on us and moved to Cornwall. He didn't want anything to do with us any more and showed a lot of hatred towards us.

When we went to see Carol my dad told us all this in great detail. Now as far as I was concerned nobody could ever have known what had taken place within our family so that was the proof that Carol is genuine. You can guess at some things but not something like that. Dad even told her of David's threat to kill us.

"Apart from his anger over this incident Dad still maintained the great sense of humour he had in life. Once my sister took some friends with her to see Carol and because they felt a bit wary they asked if Susie would sit in with them. As soon as they had sat down dad came through.

"Carol said 'I think this is your Dad, Sue.'

"So Sue said 'Dad I'm very sorry, I love you very much but I've come with Sarah today."

"Dad then said, in a precise, polite way so typical of him, "Oh I'm terribly sorry, please accept my apologies,' and left.

"After my dad died my mum really wasn't in a good place. Her health was good but she really wanted to be with dad. But she knew she had us and her grandchildren so stayed strong for that reason. Eventually with age her health did deteriorate and she developed chest problems and had difficulty breathing. Then she had a bad fall and ended up in hospital. After a week the staff couldn't understand how she was surviving.

"The amount of drugs your mum's on, if we gave them to someone else it would kill them,' the nurse said. 'Why won't your mum let go.'

"We kept saying to mum 'Go to dad. Go to dad. When he comes, go.'

"You could see in her eyes she wanted to go but there was something holding her back. Now she always said she didn't want to die in hospital. She either wanted to die in her own home or in St Giles' Hospice, Lichfield, which she had helped to set up. So we moved her there and once she was there it was almost as if a silk sheet had been lifted off her and she slipped away. However before she went she did manage to tell us that dad had come for her. Something Carol has always told us happens. In fact my dad nearly died once before his end did come. He always told us that he saw his mum. He thought she had come to get him but then turned and walked away. At that moment he revived.

"There was still the issue with my brother. I eventually managed to trace an email address for him and sent a message saying that mum had passed away. As it was during Covid we were only allowed 10 people at the funeral. So I told him this and that the crematorium wanted the names and addresses of all the people who were attending within 24 hours. I received no reply. So 24 hours later I told him that the offer to attend would have to be withdrawn. I think he thought it was me being awkward because he then telephoned the crematorium and told them he was coming and he implied he was going to cause trouble of a violent nature. A cousin of mine arranged some bodyguides that she knew of to act as an insurance, to be there just in case. But it was just an idle threat. He didn't turn up.

"We then worried about going to see Carol because if mum was not there with dad it sort of blew a hole in all we believe in. But we went and as I sat down in Carol's kitchen she gasped.

"Oh that was powerful,' she said. 'There's two people here and I think they might be your mum and dad.'

"I didn't need to know anything else. I was happy. Carol went on to say how mum had passed but that she was fine again. She could breathe again and life was back to normal because she was with dad. She even said all the Golden Retrievers they'd had were with them. She then spoke of the funeral and the threats my brother had made. So again, how could anybody guess at that.

"So through a period of 18 or 19 years we have seen Carol so many times as a family and she has told us things that have always been such a comfort, particularly for my mum.

"They were both cremated which is what they wanted. Originally dad wanted his ashes scattered in a place called Cemetery Beach in Aberdovey where they had a house. But we decided against that because mum sold the house. So we had his ashes interred in the graveyard at King's Bromley Church where they lived. And through Carol he told us that that was against his wishes. He said he wasn't happy. Although he did like the daffodils you could see.

"I never give Carol any clues. She might say something and add 'does that mean anything to you?' but I'll just tell her to carry on. I mark it with an asterisk so I can tell her later she's right. At the end she'll say 'so what was that there,' and I tell her. Then she'll say 'well that was really interesting.' I find that a positive thing.

"Carol once told me that spirit can choose to be where they want to be in their lives and that my mum and dad are in their forties. She has also told me that they are often sitting by my shoulder.

"She always comes up with numbers and dates. She always mentions the 9 March 2003 which is the date my dad died. But now she also mentions the day mum died – 12 May 2020. She'll say I've got 9 and 12 and March and May and 2003 and 2020. Then she'll say 'I'm a bit confused because everything begins with M. But I think it's the 9 March 2003 and the 12 May 2020. Now nobody could know that. And if they could, why would they know it?

"Then she comes up with names. She told my sister she could see two children – Lauren and Elliot. She said you're worried about Elliott. I can see a big hospital. Something to do with xrays. Lauren works as a radiographer at the Queen Elizabeth in Birmingham.

"I can't stress enough how impressive Carol is. She doesn't really want praise, it's not why she does it. But for Susie and myself the most comforting thing for Susie and myself is that both mum and dad understand my feelings towards my brother, or lack of feelings, and his hatred of me. But most of all is that they are together. Because if they hadn't been it would have put a question on all we believe in.

A Ruthin Castle resident that is not a spirit

The grounds of the castle and a red object in the distance which wasn't there. What is it?

William Cornwallis-West. Once owner of Ruthin Castle.

My husband Steve who everyone says looks like the Colonel

Our wedding in the castle

No matter how often the walls are painted,
the jug remains

The hallway in Ruthin Castle

The banqueting hall in Ruthin Castle

The dog in the mirror at the
Manor House in Tamworth

A meeting with an extraordinary woman

I once had a lady come for a reading who afterwards asked if I would see her daughter.

"Yes of course I will," I said.

She hesitated before continuing. "I don't know whether you will want to see her."

"Why not?" I asked.

"There may be a problem because you're a white witch aren't you?"

"Well so I'm told," I said. "And I do like to class myself as a white witch because I don't think I'm a bad person. But then I've never met a black witch to compare."

"Well that's the problem," she said. "My daughter is a black witch."

"Oh I see," I said starting to feel a bit concerned. "Well good and bad don't really mix."

"Exactly. But she desperately wants to see you."

"Ok but can I think about it first?"

"Tell you what," she suggested. "How about if I book eight months in advance. Then I'll check with you nearer the time."

So I booked her in under her normal name, then forgot about it. Three weeks prior to the reading I got a phone call from the mother, reminding me I was getting a visit from her daughter. I didn't click at first because names don't mean anything to me. But then she reminded me that this was the girl who was a black witch.

"Oh," I said. "That has come round so quick?"

I couldn't really understand why she wanted to come and see me. From what I've heard about black witches they're evil people. So what good would it do her, having me give her a reading? But something clicked in my head and I thought, what have you got lose. So I agreed but said that if I felt uncomfortable at any time, or she felt uncomfortable, we would have to stop.

"Well she's coming for specific reasons and she feels she needs to talk to you." I was told. "You won't believe me if I tell you, but she can listen in and you'll just think it's mad."

It all sounded very eerie at the time, but I certainly don't think it's mad now..

A few days later I went to my local hardware store for some paint and while I was there got talking to the manager whose name was Clare.

"You're the medium aren't you?" she asked. Adding – "If I give you my staff discount will you do me a reading?

"Of course I will." I said. "Thank you very much."

So I booked her in for the 7th of October, the same day the black witch was due to come. Clare's booking was for after I had given the witch her reading, although it would mean I would be giving four readings that morning, so warned her I might not be as fully responsive as normal. She said she didn't mind. She just wanted to give it a go.

On the 6th of October the witch phoned me up.

"Is that Carol?"

"Yes."

She told me who she was and I admitted to being a little bit nervous.

"Well don't be," she said. "Anyway I'm just checking everything is scheduled for tomorrow as I shall be travelling from Shropshire."

"Yes."

"Ok I'll see you tomorrow."

She put the phone down and I thought how nice she sounded.

The next morning it dawned on me that Clare might not have got my address. So I phoned her up.

"Oh Carol," she said. "I'm so glad you phoned me the most weirdest thing has happened. I haven't got any staff. They're all off sick so I can't come. But I do want to come so please can I have another date."

Which I gave her. Then just after I'd put the phone down it rang. It was the witch.

"Just letting you know I shall be a wee tad early." she said.

"Oh that's fine. You can sit and wait in the lounge while I finish with the person before you."

This was no problem because it used to happen all the time before Covid. I was always still with someone when my next reading arrived.

I was about to put the phone down when she continued.

"And when you have finished with my session, maybe, we can move on to your session."

"Pardon?"

"I need to talk to you. And don't worry your next reading isn't coming. I've made sure she has no staff in the business."

Well I nearly dropped the phone. I couldn't think how she knew that.

Then she said – "And if you're working before me you might find it a wee strange."

My first reading arrived and it was horrific. I was looking at her but all I could see was this young man hanging from a noose. Then I started to feel really sick. I went to ask her if the young man meant anything to her. But as I started everything went blank and all I could hear was this woman's voice saying – "Carol? Carol?"

I was going down this lane where it was just dusty and nothing there apart from trees. It was really hot so I didn't think I was in England, unless it was in the summer. Then there was an old farmhouse. I reached the door, opened it and went in. It was like I was in a dream. I saw the most amazing Jacobean staircase and thought "Oh this is absolutely fabulous!" Then I saw a door. It was like a stable door, cut in half where there is a latch on either piece to get through. So I opened the door and as I did all I could smell was death and then this thing just threw me back. I quickly shut the door and then I was back in my kitchen and doing my reading.

"Oh Carol," she said. "It was like you were really spaced out."

I asked her if she knew anyone who owned a farmhouse or similar. But she said no and that she had no idea what I was talking about.

That reading finished and my second one arrived. Again I didn't really get anything and again I felt really spaced out. I apologised telling her I was nervous because I just didn't know what was going to greet me at the door when my next reading arrived.

The witch didn't arrive early so I waited nervously and then there was a knock on my door. When I opened it I couldn't believe my eyes. There was this woman, in her thirties, with the pentagon painted on her face and a dowser in her hand. I could feel my adrenalin rising.

She told me she was pleased to meet me, but added – "Well, we'll see when we get inside."

As she walked in, all I noticed were her shoes. They were a really strange colour. She took them off and left them in the porch, then stood in the door way and began waving the dowser. As she did her voice changed as she kept repeating "nice, nice, nice" as she moved through the room. Although on a couple of occasions she did shout out – "deceit!"

Eventually she reached the wall where a large picture of me and Steve, taken when we renewed our wedding vows, hangs. She put her hand on it and made a grunting noise then said – "Is that your husband?"

Rather stupidly I said – "Well yes I've got my wedding dress on."

With that she quickly turned to face me saying – "don't be sarcastic!"

Placing her hand back on the picture she asked "Why has your husband not had any teeth for months?"

"What?" I said.

"Don't question me!" she retorted. "Why has he no teeth?"

"Well they keep breaking and he's having dental treatment at the moment and has had to have some out."

"And why does he walk with a limp?"

"Because he had a thrombosis."

I didn't know what to say but then she took her hand away from the picture and said, "We're going in there aren't we?" pointing to the kitchen.

So we went in and she sat down opposite me and just stared at me.

She was a most remarkable looking woman and had got really long finger nails, almost like talons. Not pointed, but squared, and they were cream with a green line painted on them.

I got the cards out and as I did she put her hand out on mine and said – "We will start with me but, we will finish with you."

As I handed her the cards for her to shuffle she said "I was told no tarot. Why do you not use the devil's cards?"

"Because I don't like them. And I don't do Ouija either, and I did ask your mum that if you'd done any Ouija before you came I couldn't have you in the house."

She looked at me. "I haven't forecast my friends for over a week. Not until I'd been to see you."

So I did her reading, which was just a normal reading, and I even made her cry.

"Nobody makes a black witch cry," she said.

Apparently I hit nerves that she said nobody had ever touched before.

"I was told you were an incredible woman." she said. "But I had to see for myself."

I then began getting the word Romania.

"Why Romania?" I asked. "Are you going to Romania?"

"Romania is my son," she said.

So trying to make light of things I said "Oh did you call him after the country."

"No I did not. I like the name."

And that was how it was. Short, sharp answers.

Then I saw the man with the noose around his neck.

"Oh can you see him?" she asked.

So I told her it wasn't the first time I'd seen him that morning.

"Yes that's right darling, but carry on."

Now I was back in the farmhouse again.

"Can you take a....."

But before I could finish she answered. "Yes I can take a farmhouse. And you've seen my Jacobean staircase haven't you? That's where I'm putting my mother and my son. The other half is my house. My house. With my people."

"The dead?"

"Correct."

She continued. "It is an old farmhouse. I bought it in Valencia."

The way she described it was that it wasn't a monastery, but it was a place which housed only males. And at some time a lot of these males hung themselves. There has been several deaths but I only actually picked up one death. That is the part in which she is going to live. She had the staircase stripped from the old part and moved to a newer bit where her mother and son are going to live. She told me she is eventually going to open it as a witch's retreat. And she's invited me over.

"But I'm a white witch," I said.

"I'm inviting you over," she repeated.

We finished the reading and she was over the moon.

"I can come back can't I?"

"Yes," I said and bent over to pick all the cards up to put them away. As I did, she grabbed a piece of my hair and pulled it out.

"Ouch!" I said.

"That's all right darling," she said, holding a clump of my hair in her hand. "I didn't hurt you."

"What's that for?" I asked.

"It's ok," she said. "It's your turn now."

I said I needed to go upstairs first. While I was upstairs I heard the back door open and when I came down discovered she had been out in my garden. She had got this little bottle, it was a lovely little bottle, and in it she had put some soil from my garden, together with my hair and some salt.

"That's not mine," I said, referring to the salt. "I don't use salt."

"Yes it is," she said. "Put it back in your cupboard."

"But it's not mine."

She didn't answer so I just did as she'd asked and it's stayed there ever since.

As she mixed the three items I asked her what it was for.

"I'll tell you in a minute."

Then she took hold of my hand and started my reading.

"This is a lovely house but there is a lot of negativity. Someone's making you ill and you need to dig your own tunnel to get out of it. He loves you but he's scared to make decisions and he doesn't listen or take things in. You're polar opposites and two different people but he's a good man who doesn't fight for what he wants. There's poison been set down and he needs to make a proper decision for both of you. But he's too scared and too laid back. You're at the point in your life where you need a complete change."

Then she gave me a warning – "He's hiding a secret. Beware of a woman with a gold tooth. She's evil."

"There's a dog in the house, over there," she said pointing to the doorway. "It's got a patch on its eye and follows your husband around."

Steve once had a dog called Butch which had a patch on its eye.

She continued with mentioning members of my family.

"You have a daughter who is ill, but not majorly and there's a small man who follows you around. Seriously ill he was. I think it was Motor-Neurone."

Steve's dad died of Motor-Neurone and although Steve is 6' 3" – his dad was only 5' 6"

"There is a woman in your life and you need to protect yourself when you see her. She turns people against people. And there's a man who wants to be trusted but there have been too many lies over the years.

"You have a sister in spirit world who was jealous of you."

As soon as she started talking about my sister I could sense she was getting puzzled.

"But I'm a bit confused," she said. "There's a bit of a mystery around you. But go with what you feel."

So I told her about my thoughts as to whether my sister was my mum. She bent forward and her whole voice changed and with a strange, rasping sound said "You'll never know the truth."

She told me of rejections I would suffer but then there would be new beginnings and I would have decisions to make.

"You're fantastic at your job and with people," she said. "But you need to not be taken for a fool any more. Even from your loved ones."

Then she leant over and said "Why do I want to say I'm here for a reason."

So I told her I was writing a book but she said she knew.

Then she went back to talk about a woman with a gold tooth and that there was a lot of deceit around her.

"I won't hurt her," she said. "But I will warn her. And if the first warning doesn't work she'll get another one. Then the third one will be worse than the second one."

I laughed and she glared at me and said, "Carol you're not taking me seriously."

"But I don't want any of this. I'm not that sort of person." I said.

"No but you deserve to have a bit of happiness."

As she was leaving she said to me – "when you come to Shropshire you'll go through my village. I will see you with the heather. And you will see a white owl on the post. White owls are your animal. If the white owl stares at you and turns its head a good degree, your gift will be six time foretold." She didn't know I was going to Shropshire but she knew.

So when Steve came home I asked him who he knew who had got a gold tooth. He went round all the women he knew at work but no one had got a gold tooth. But one woman has got a gold bar through the middle of her tongue.

A couple of weeks later, one Monday, I was in the nursery and all of a sudden I got this headache. The girls were worried because I went grey and all I could keep saying was "my head, my head." It lasted for five minutes and I remembered the time. It was 12.22pm.

Steve came home that night and said that a woman at work, the one who has a little gold bar in her tongue, had had an accident. She'd split her head open. I asked him what time it had happened although I knew exactly what he was going to say. It was at around 12.20pm.

Then we went on our trip to Shropshire. We weren't able to stay at our usual place so we were up on the moor in a little village just outside Knighton. It was quite a foggy day when we arrived but, because we were early, we decided to have a drive around the moor to kill time before we checked in. We were driving along a quiet road and were surprised to see a white van which seemed to be parked in a strange place. Driving on a bit further we then decided to turn around as it was getting near the time to check in to our accommodation. As we went back down the road we noticed this van was still there. Then we saw her. Walking up the moor with heather in her hand. I remember noticing that she hadn't got the pentagon painted on her face. Steve stopped the car and we both got out. But she had disappeared. And so had the van.

"She can transport herself anywhere." I said.

Later we went to a local pub in the village and I was speaking to the young barmaid there called Rosie. And Steve happened to say "isn't there a witch who lives around here."

"Yes but we're not sure where. We think she's in the old chapel at the bottom of the lane. But nobody ever sees her. But we're all warned that if we get someone knocking on the door not to open it. How did you know?"

"Well somebody came to see me from Shropshire." I said and told her about it.

"We call her the Black Witch of the Village." Rosie continued. "And my Dad always used to say, if ever this woman knocks on the door don't answer the door."

Then she told us a story about her dad. He once had an accident and was in hospital in an induced coma. His chances were quite slim. One evening someone knocked on her door so Rosie went to open it and there standing on her doorstep was the witch.

"Oh my dear," she said. "My van's broken down and I don't have a mobile phone could I use your phone?"

Rosie said she was scared but decided to let her in. After she had finished her call she turned to Rosie and said, "you'll have a phone call in ten minutes."

"Who from?"

"From your father. Goodbye." And left.

Ten minutes later her phone went and it was her dad. He'd come out of his coma the previous hour and was fine. Rosie said she couldn't believe it. And although her dad was furious she'd let the witch in, she told him that she really felt that she, the witch, had helped him.

A few weeks later we were staying in Longnor, as we do every year before Christmas to visit the market at Chatsworth. On the evening we went to the pub called the Winking Man as we always do. As always it was a lovely meal. On the way back Steve suddenly stopped the car and was just staring out of the window. As I turned my head there was a white owl perched on a post just a few feet away. It did a thirty degree turn and just stared at me. It didn't move, it didn't fly off, it just sat staring at me. I'll never forgot looking into the eyes of that owl and strangely, since seeing that, things have been coming into my head faster than they ever have before.

When we came home the witch phoned me up and even before I answered the phone, I knew it was her.

"I knew it was you," I said.

"Yes, because I've got into your head now," she said. "And I'm in your head until we put you right. Because meeting you was one of my most fascinating experiences in life."

"Well meeting you was one of mine."

"I'll be absolutely honest," she continued. "I thought I'd knock you down because I'm evil and you're good. And evil and good don't work."

I asked her if it was her on the moors.

"Yes it was."

"You didn't have the pentagon painted on your face?"

"No I didn't, because the pentagon was there to protect me from you when I came to see you."

"You don't need protecting from me," I said.

"They say good and bad don't mix, but that's a load of farce. You're good, I'm bad, we mix."

She told me she doesn't eat any of our food. She wouldn't even have a glass of water. She often drinks her own urine and makes everything herself. In a cauldron. Outside. And she makes all her own clothes and all her own remedies. She's never been to a doctor in her life. And says she will never step foot in a hospital. Her mother is a white witch but she said her son is untouched. Just a normal little boy. I asked her if he ever saw his dad and she said "no, he's the devil's child.' I didn't ask any more but I know that people do do all sorts of rituals and things.

She said she uses everything by sevens and later I bought a scratch card. I don't know why because I've never bought one before but I just felt I needed to. The numbers all included a seven in them and I won £50.

But it was the way her voice kept changing. And her eyes. I've never seen eyes like it. They were huge and appeared blue but then changed to grey. I was just mesmerised by her eyes.

She really is the most fascinating person I have ever met. In the whole of my life I have never met such an incredible woman. And I'm so pleased I agreed to see her as I am now a much stronger person since I met her. I sincerely believe in everything I do, and I know there is also bad out there. But from what I've seen now, demonic isn't as bad as people make out. She's protects. She is a protector in a sense. And when I think about it there have been times since meeting her that I've shouted at someone. Something I've never done before, but I've felt I've been goaded to do it. But my shouting has eased an atmosphere, not only between myself and the other person, but also those around us too. So although I felt I was doing something bad at the time, good had actually come from my actions.

Since that short interlude I have never seen this woman again........but I know she's out there somewhere.

Spirit guiding my pen

All through this book I have spoken about things of the past. But while writing this book I experienced many things which seemed to tie in with the writing of the book. Almost as if spirit was trying to inspire me, that they wanted me to write this book.

I started writing this book in 2021. After Christmas of that year we went on a short break to Dacre Park in Driffield. It is a place I really love to go and has been a favourite of mine for many years. It totally relaxes me as it's on a lake and I love being by water. Sitting by this lake and watching the wildlife really inspired me as I wrote this book. It's amazing what being by water does. It's like a constant therapy. Like everyone, I needed this holiday to just sit and think about the future, which will bring about new beginnings. Steve losing his job after forty-five years, from boy to man, will certainly be a new beginning.

I don't know whether spirit was encouraging me but every night we heard strange noises. Once while sitting on the edge of the couch I could hear tapping, or rattling noises, every time I put pen to paper. Other things kept happening too.

On the first night the shower in the master bedroom came on, all on its own. It was down the corridor from where we were sitting in the lounge but we heard it.

Steve said "Is that water?"

"Have you left the tap running," I asked.

So he went and looked and came back saying "the shower's on."

The television kept switching channels. One evening we were watching Carry On Henry during which I got up to go and get a drink. At the same time Steve got up to go and have a cigarette. While we were away the television went off.

I said to Steve – "You've switched the television off."

"Carol I haven't." he said.

So I went to get the remote and when I switched the television back on, it switched to a different channel.

On the last night we were both in the hot tub, which is positioned on a long balcony. The light switches for this balcony are inside the lodge, but all of a sudden all the lights came on.

Steve said "How's that happened? Impossible you need to flick the switch."

When we checked the switch – it had been switched on. Every night we heard noises in that hot tub but on that last night we saw two shooting stars too. I think it was my energy making it all happen because I was concentrating on writing my book.

That New Years Eve we spent in the clubhouse. It was a wonderful night. It can be difficult for me when I go to parties because I see all these spirits around the people there. New Year's Eve is a special night so I sat and watched. There were so many sprits around. All loving the people they were with and happy to be with them. When we were doing Auld Lang Syne I could see dozens of hands crossing over each individual. Someone came up and made me get up and dance. But while we danced there was a lady at his side. As he twirled me around I kept seeing her face in front of me. I then found out he had not long lost his wife. She was there and as I was being spun round she was watching us.

While I was at Dacre Park I had two dreams. The first dream was about my sister. In the dream she had a shop and it was broken in to. There were two men and they were on the floor. They talked about silicon. The floor had gaps in it running from side to side where stones were being thrown in. My dream book says the shop represents a stroke of luck but the robbery means I must be careful how I handle money. Dreaming of my sister means domestic disagreements. And changes with the floor means obligations to an on-going situation. The stones being thrown mean a regret over a missed opportunity and a lesson to be learnt.

My second dream included Steve's mum and dad and his brother Adrian, who was dressed for a marathon in a ruby and green outfit, carrying some coloured fruit. I couldn't make out what the fruit was, just that there were lots of colours. The bannister broke in the house and my yellow towel in the bathroom was missing, which really upset me. I was trying to keep it together but couldn't. Someone was telling my fortune and then I was driving. I don't even drive but I reversed the car into a wire fence. Steve was in the car with me and was building with lego bricks and there were bags with two loaves of bread on the back seat.

Dreaming of your house means renewal of old associates. My father-in-law, who actually spoke to me, means important news and seeing my brother-in-law, who is gay, ready to do a marathon wearing the vivid ruby and green and holding the fruit, means domestic security. It also signifies a life with domestic comfort but not great luxury. The colour green pertains to travel, or news of a renewal, and my saying that my yellow towel was missing shows comfort and joy to come. The car reversing means recovering something lost, and the bread indicates security. The plastic bag means friendship for life. So when you put it all together it does add up to my life.

A couple of months later we were back in Ruthin.

The visit there this time seemed very special. As usual as soon as I saw the castle I had that feeling which I can't explain. I'm like a child who gets butterflies when something exciting is happening and I get this feeling that I'm home. But this time I got it more than ever before. I was sobbing by the time I got to the castle and Steve was saying "Oh Carol what on earth's going on." But I couldn't explain it. Ruthin is just the most magical place in the whole world. And what made it even more emotional was that when we got there, the girls were all waiting to welcome us. It was so lovely, absolutely fabulous. And I have to say that the castle was more active than it's ever been. Particularly on the Sunday evening. You could hear children laughing, adults having fun. It just felt like it was party time for the spirits.

After we had arrived we went to the White Horse which is on the outskirts of Ruthin for dinner. A place we often visit while staying at the castle. An old coaching inn it is actually attached to a church so the grounds of the pub form part of the churchyard. As we sat there, eating our lunch, I noticed a shadow at my side. At the same time Steve heard a ladies voice right by his ear which made him jump and unnerved him a bit. He described it as a grunt, or a cough, but no words uttered. The shadow remained with me for the whole of my meal.

I asked Keith, the owner, and he said that other customers had seen things and he had experienced glasses being moved from the shelves. He said nothing bad had ever happened in the pub although one of his staff members once felt she was being pushed while on the staircase. But he only ever felt good and happiness there, nothing bad at all.

Afterwards we went back to castle and did our usual looking around, which we love to do. We went down to the Mediaeval Banquet Hall and just sat there. A very old part of the castle its fireplace dates back to Henry V's era, so being in there is really like stepping back in time. After a while I went to the toilet and left Steve on his own. When I came back he looked like he'd seen a ghost. He was sitting at one of the tables on a long wooden bench when he felt someone lean on the table and it creaked. When he looked up he saw a shadow run past him. It stopped at the opposite side of the bench and for once he did feel scared and went really cold, freezing cold. He didn't move, he just sat there, waiting for me to come back from the toilet. The shadow just stayed there, not moving, until I walked through the door and then it just disappeared.

Close to the Banquet Hall is an old staircase. You can see how much it has been used over the years and it is quite eerie. Sometimes you can sense a feeling of being watched but this time I did see a man. He was wearing a soldiers outfit made of mesh and wore a huge metal glove on his right hand. I'd never seen him before in all the years I've been going there. He was looking directly over my shoulder, but behind him was a lady in the blue dress. They didn't stay there for long and we went back to our room. Going in we found all the lights were on but I know that when we had left earlier I made sure they were switched off.

This wasn't the first time the lady in the blue dress has been seen. One of the staff members was passing room 222 one day when he heard someone crying. The door was open, so he went in, and found a lady in a blue dress was in there. He asked her if she was all right.

"I'm very well thank you," she said.

He asked if she'd like anything but she said, "No I'm fine thank you."

He thought it was strange as she sounded very old fashioned but he left the room and shut the door behind him.

As he was concerned about her he went straight to reception and said "We'll have to keep an eye on room 222 as there's a lady in there whose crying."

The others looked at each and said "But there's nobody staying in 222."

So he went back up and found the room empty. There was no one there, nothing.

On the walls of the staircase leading back to the reception there are numerous pictures. As he went passed one of them he heard her voice say – "That's me."

When he looked he saw a picture of the lady in the blue dress. After that the picture strangely disappeared and no one knew where it had gone until one day when it turned up in Jenny's Room, room 222.

That afternoon we got chatting to a couple called Gavin and Emma who had asked if they could sit at the chairs close by us. As we talked we discovered they were there to celebrate his birthday. Emma said she was really interested in history so Steve offered to take them around and show them all the bits of history connected to the hotel. She was absolutely fascinated with everything. We met up in the bar again later and I told them what I did and that I was getting feelings about them.

I told Emma that her grandmother was with her and when I mentioned her name she said I was right about that. Then I mentioned there was a gentleman with her grandmother called Andy. She knew exactly who that was. But then I found myself reading Gavin – I could read him like a book.

He said he didn't believe in anything like that, saying it was all a load of rubbish. But I looked at him and said "You haven't grieved."

Taken aback for a moment he then nodded, and then he opened up and all his emotions came out. He said he had never expressed himself in such a way before. Being in the army meant he was quite a tough guy and having seen what he'd seen he couldn't grieve for his mum and felt guilty.

He said he felt guilty because his mum had died and he was blaming himself for it but couldn't understand why. She had said she loved him just before she died but he still felt guilty because he had chosen the army over her and that they hadn't really spoken a lot when they were together.

"God you don't know me," he said, "but you have just put the whole of my life out in about ten minutes. I came to a castle for my birthday and wasn't expecting to get the whole of my life story. It's the best birthday I've ever had."

He said he'd always wanted an answer as to why he felt guilty and had even been to see counsellors. But now after talking to me he felt so fulfilled and we have remained good friends ever since.

We met up with them again on another visit. I'd mentioned to the staff they were coming so they were given the room opposite to us. After we'd been for a drink Gavin went back up to their room to fetch something and discovered the television had been switched on. I have known people who have stayed in that room before and said the television kept coming on.

There was also a couple who were on honeymoon who loved history and so we took them down to see the Medieval room. And then to the King Edward room. This room has the oldest fireplace in the castle. It's a magnificent room with a large old, very old, ornate wooden door. Usually this room is never locked but no matter how hard I tried I couldn't get in. The door just wouldn't open. I tried several times, pushing, twisting and turning the handle and pulling but to no avail. Even the man with me, who was a large man, couldn't move it. So, deciding it must be locked, I went rushing back to reception to get a key. They were surprised it was locked because no one had ever had to use the key before. As they handed me this huge, old iron key I looked at it and must have seemed puzzled because they laughed.

"You're down in the twelfth century bit there," they said.

So back I went, put the key in the door and before I could do anything the door flew open.

The following day was Steve's birthday and we sat in the lobby watching the world go by. It's such a peaceful place to get your head around things and it's almost as if things are put in your head.

When Steve finished work after being made redundant it wasn't easy at our ages but things happen for a reason. Hopefully this will be a new chapter. And where best to sort our lives out but at Ruthin. We were inspired just sitting in the chairs and it was like a new lease of life. I never ask for anything in my life but I did. I asked in my head what the future held for us and two things happened. The knob on the library bar door moved a couple of times. It was locked both sides as nobody was in there but as we watched it we could see a shadow through the gap under the door where the sun shone through. It was like someone was walking on the other side of the door. There was only the two of us sitting there but then both of us felt as if someone was walking around us.

On the Sunday night we went down into the Medieval room again. Over the previous weeks they had held an event in there dedicated to Harry Potter so there were lots of wizardry-type decorations in there. The temperatures were constantly changing. Steve asked out but I told him to be careful.

"Please would it be possible to show yourself or make a noise," he said. "You know we're not here to hurt you. I've been coming here for over thirty years and I'd like to meet you."

It went really cold and we heard a couple of creaks. Above us on the beam, left there from the witches and wizards theme night, there were shields which were attached by chicken wire. They were hanging quite normally and perfectly secure. One was green with a black snake on, like a serpent. The middle one had a peacock on it and at the other end was a shield with a white owl on it. Steve continued saying how much he loved the place and that he thought he might be part of the family.

"Just show me that you agree with what we are doing," he asked.

Suddenly it was like the chicken wire had been cut and the shield with the snake on just floated down off the beam onto floor behind Steve. It was like someone was guiding it down. None of the others were moving. Nothing in that room was moving – nothing. Just as this happened one of the cleaners came past and couldn't believe what was happening and said that they had been up for weeks.

"That's the most weirdest thing I've seen in my life," she said. "I hope you don't mind but I was standing at the door watching."

"Weird?" said Steve. "I can't tell you what it's done to me."

As I've said I never, ever, ask out. It's against all my principles. But the symbol of the snake worried me because I couldn't help thinking it usually represents something bad. So I said, "Please," to the white owl on the end, "Please just show me your face. Please I'm not here to hurt you. I don't want to hurt anybody by doing this. This is totally disrespectful, and I know I never do it, but I just need to know that everything is all right."

With that the owl shield spun right around to look me straight in the face. Even I was speechless. It just hung there staring at me. The other one hadn't moved. There were also three broomsticks hanging up and they hadn't moved either so it couldn't have been because there was a draft in there. If there had been a gust of wind through an open window or door they all would have moved.

All the time we were in that Medieval room it was like we were being watched. Even Steve said it's like there are eyes on us everywhere. That's the first time I've ever really felt that. I didn't feel anything bad. If anything I felt good about it.

During that stay we walked across the bridge for the very first time in thirty-four years. It spans the old moat and, until it was renovated, had been totally impassable. It is where the Lady Grey is often seen walking. It did feel strange, standing on the bridge, and very eerie. We've spent many times looking at it and standing underneath it, but never walked it. We walked it on the night and I have to admit my nerves would only let me get halfway across.

During that stay I spent quite a bit of time in the lobby, writing my book. The whole atmosphere changed when we sat down and all the time I felt that I was being watched constantly. It was like having a pair of eyes attached to my back. The whole time I felt I was being goaded to carry on writing to the end and so many things were coming into my head. I was writing furiously and felt I was constantly being watched – but in a nice way. Hanging over me were the portraits of Cornwallis and his wife Patsy and I could feel his eyes on me.

Normally when we are there we go out somewhere in the car everyday but this weekend we just stayed there. It was really quite bizarre.

Over the three nights we were there we heard knocking on the door. It happens quite often when we're there but not as much as this time. It was constant and Friday was the worst. It only lasted for five minutes but it felt like eternity. Steve wanted to open the door but I said no. The knocking came from the lower level of the door. Not the normal spot someone would knock on a door. Afterwards I found out that there's a little girl who they call Tye. A member of staff has seen her and it's been noted that she always knocks on Lillie Langtrey's door, which is the room we always have. They're not sure who she is but in the offices there is a picture of a little girl in a blue dress wearing a hat and carrying a basket. Which is the image of the little girl Steve once saw floating in mid air.

After Steve's redundancy we wanted to become caretakers at a camping site. It would have been wonderful except for one thing – the accommodation we were going to be living in. I'd spotted this small building on a previous visit there and every time I looked at it, a face was peering out of the window at me. I mentioned it to the owner but he said the place was empty. However he was to tell me later that someone had lived there, but had also died in there, from Covid. So when he told me that that, would be where we would live, I just couldn't do it.

So our life goes on. There will be many more experiences and many more people to meet but in this moment I just want to feel I have done some good and given people hope. So to end I'd like to say a massive big thank you to all past and present at Ruthin Castle that has made this possible for me. It is the most magical place to be. Full of history and a place full of love and respect. It gave me the inspiration to write this book and is the place where I first knew I had to do something about telling my story.

I hope everyone enjoys the book and I hope it gives comfort to some people. Those who are sceptic I hope it will open some of your eyes. There is always someone around us just wishing to help even though we don't know it. Also as one door closes, another door opens. To me it's a circle of life to death and then we go around and around again all leaving different knowledge and ways, some exciting, some upsetting. But as I say we all have to learn lessons and as the title of my book says – we're all here for a reason. In this world there is control, nastiness, hurt, tears, loneliness or other massive things in people's lives, there are very few people who witness only good. But we are all learning lessons and curbs.

I would like to say a massive thank you to Vanessa who is an absolute wonderful person. She has taken all my memories and put them in some kind of order and has become a friend for life. Our conversations have inspired me and given me this opportunity to tell everyone of my experiences and my strange life.

I'd also like to thank everyone at Dacre Park too. This wonderful area by the water also helped give me the inspiration to clear my head and remember past events.

Finally I would like to thank everyone who reads about my life and spirit world. And to tell you that if it happens to you it isn't anything bad like witchcraft. Please go with it. No one can change why we are here. As the title says – we are here from a reason. So please don't be scared. Remember there is life out there, we don't just go to nothing. And yes we do meet up with our loved ones and life goes round in circles. We are all learning lessons and goals and nothing in anyone's life is easy. Love, money, success or poverty, no matter what diversity or ethnicity we are, we are all the same. One soul, just here for different reasons and different goals.

While writing this book I had a lady walk in and say to me "I'm here for a reason." I couldn't believe what I was hearing and just looked at her.

"That's what my book's going to be called," I said.

She said she was here for a reason and it was for her dad to come through. She'd been to see a few mediums and he'd never come through before. She said that before she'd come into the house she had sat in the car pleading with him to come through.

"I'm not asking you," she had said to him. "I'm telling you."

Her father had been a total unbeliever but to her delight he did come through. On that morning I had certainly been there for a reason and she went away happy.

One final experience

With the book finished came the long wait to publish it. During that time Steve and I did start having problems. And there were more problems with the house. Everything was getting on top of me. I was heading for a breakdown. I'd actually said I'd had enough of spirit world. I didn't want to do it any more. I just felt I'd had so many problems and no one was ever there for me. But I also felt I couldn't do it any more. That I'd lost whatever I had. I even told Steve to throw my cards in the bin.

"Nothing ever goes right for us." I'd said. "There's only so much bad luck one person, or two people can take. We're selling the house and we're leaving. Or you go on your own."

And that's how it had got.

We needed a break, so decided to visit Longnor and while there we went over to the Winking Man. This time we weren't put at our usual table but close to one of the fire doors which is never open. It's a really heavy door but all of a sudden it started to open. When I looked, there was nothing there. Steve had got his back to it so asked if I could see anything.

"No," I said. "But I feel really funny."

I looked away for a second then, when I looked up again, I could see a man standing at the door. He was all in black and staring at me with these vivid blue eye. I couldn't see his face. Just his eyes.

The landlord then appeared saying – "What's happened to my door? That's not possible!"

A short while later I went to the toilet. As I was washing my hands I lifted my head and looked in the mirror. And there he was. Standing behind me. That same man without a face but with the same piercing blue eyes. He reached out and put his hand on my shoulder. It felt really heavy.

"What do you want?" I asked. But he didn't answer and just disappeared.

When I got back to the table, Steve looked at me and said – "you look like you're seen a ghost."

"I have," I said.

"What happened?"

"I don't know Steve but I feel so different. Really different."

Later that evening I became really emotional. I couldn't stop crying and Steve and I sat down and talked like we've never talked before.

When we got back home we both felt so different. The house felt so different. It was like something had been lifted. And I said to Steve that this was like a positive thing. Later I realised that things I normally got quite uptight about just didn't bother me anymore. I've no idea who that man was but he gave me the weirdest experience I've ever had in all my paranormal times.

It had only been the week before we left for Landor that I had thought of giving it all up so this was almost like they were saying please Carol – don't. And now I can just feel they're there for me. I can feel someone following me around all the time.

A couple of months later we were back in Ruthin Castle and it was like they knew we were coming. As we walked into our usual room, Lily's room, the door slammed shut behind us with such a bang. Unusual because it always sticks and has to be shut manually.

"Oh they know we're back," said Steve, laughing.

Then the lights were going on and off in synchronisation.

I looked around and said "Come on guys I never ask you for anything but please give me something." But after that everything seemed quiet. Until the last day.

We were sat in a small room called the snug. There's only two chairs in there which look out through a window. So we sat there having a quiet drink. After a while I noticed the shadow of a man by a post and thought he was probably waiting to see if we were ready to leave so he could have our seats. As I turned round to see who it was, there was a soldier standing there with those same bright blue piercing eyes and lovely smile. This time I could see his face. He appeared an older man and he had a massive beam on his face. It was the most beautiful caring smile I've ever seen. He appeared to be wearing a dress made of chain mail with a matching hood and shoes which matched the suit of armour. I turned away for a second then when I looked back he'd gone but he left me feeling totally comforted.

Finishing our drinks we decided to go on our usual walk-about. As we went down one of the corridors we could both hear a noise. I stood outside the door which used to lead into the tea rooms, but which was now being used a store room, and went to open the door but realised it was locked. As I took my hand away I could see the door handle starting to turn. First it turned one way then it turned the other. Then as Steve looked down the corridor he could see numerous orbs floating up and down.

Afterwards I became so emotional again and couldn't stop crying. This was so unlike me but it has given me hope for the future. I've never had a guide, or certainly never felt I have one, but now I feel him with me all the time. I can feel the difference. I don't feel on my own and the house feels different too. I can't explain how different the house feels. And it is certainly a more positive vibe than a negative vibe.

~~ The End ~~

www.ingramcontent.com/pod-product-compliance
Lightning Source LLC
Chambersburg PA
CBHW042139160426
43201CB00021B/2337